THE ATLAS OF THE
NEW AGE

● ● ● ● ● ● ● ● ● ● ● ● ● ●

GERRY McGUIRE THOMPSON

BARRON'S

D1165279

A QUARTO BOOK

Copyright © 1999 Quarto Inc.

First edition for the United States,
its territories and dependencies
and Canada
published in 1999 by
Barron's Educational Series, Inc.

All inquiries should be addressed to:
Barron's Eductional Series, Inc.
250 Wireless Boulevard,
Hauppage, NY 11788
http://www.barronseduc.com

Library of Congress Catalog Card
No.: 99-63487
International Standard Book
No.: 0 7641 5197 5

This book was designed and produced by
Quarto Publishing plc
6 Blundell Street
London N7 9BH

Editor *Judith Samuelson*
Art Editor *Elizabeth Healey*
Copy Editor *Gill Harvey*
Designer *James Laurence*
Photographer *Paul Forrester*
Illustrators *Chen Ling, David Kemp*
Cartographer *Julian Baker*
Picture Researcher *Laurent Boubounelle*

Art Director *Moira Clinch*
Publisher *Piers Spence*

Manufactured in Hong Kong by
Regent Publishing Services Ltd
Printed in China by
Leefung-Asco Printers Ltd

THE ATLAS OF THE
NEW AGE

ASIA 76

INDIA 118

AUSTRALASIA AND THE PACIFIC 176

AFRICA AND EGYPT 100

CHINA AND JAPAN 138

This book tells the extraordinary tale of man's age-old search for the means to transform mind, body, and spirit, to walk free of the shackles of mortality, and to heal the hurts of the human condition. This atavistic longing originates in the first stirrings of human consciousness, and spans the entire planet, from the frozen poles, through the mountains, prairies, and deserts, to the equatorial rainforests. It belongs as much to simple tribal societies as to highly sophisticated civilizations, both ancient and modern.

Here you'll find an overview of the whole story, evoking the present and past with the aid of rich visual images from all over the world. You'll see an amazingly intricate pattern of coherence and interconnectedness, demonstrating how closely New Age thinking is allied to the most ancient spiritual traditions.

SIMILAR WISDOMS

One of the intriguing facets of spiritual beliefs and practices is their coherence and similarity, even in populations thousands of miles or kilometers apart with no known historical contact. Throughout the book, these interconnected traditions are highlighted in mini-features under the heading Similar Wisdoms.

ENVIRONMENTAL CONCERNS

At the heart of the New Age Movement is a deep
concern for the natural world – a sense of communion
with the planet that sees it as a living, breathing biosphere
deserving care and respect, rather than a giant
playground to be exploited at will. The tree, with its roots
deep in the earth, its crown in the air, exchanging spent
breath for life-giving oxygen in symbiosis with animal life, is
a powerful symbol of New Age consciousness.

The Spirit of the New Age

The phrase "New Age" is not always clearly understood. In practice, it is an umbrella term that covers a wide range of interests and activities, with a defined set of unifying principles. Its primary strand is the pursuit of health and harmony in a holistic way, stressing the equal importance of mind, body, and spirit. Within this, it embraces a wide range of therapies and self-help techniques, and places strong emphasis on bringing spiritual awareness and traditions into everyday life. On a broader scale, its approach involves a concern for the environment, the future of the human race, and the planet.

New Age culture began as a popular movement in the 1960s, although its roots can be discerned in the nineteenth century. Until recently, it was seen by many as insignificant and eccentric. In recent years, however, it has grown into a powerful influence on mainstream society throughout the world.

The concept of the New Age is based on patterns of cosmic influence over major periods of time. Humanity is currently moving into the Age of Aquarius, a 2100-year era associated with the cyclic tilting of the earth's axis. The last New Age, the Age of Pisces, began around the time of the birth of Christ. At points such as this, there is a tendency to recognize that our prevailing values are no longer valid, and that a radical change of direction is required. This new consciousness begins with an avant-garde movement, and gradually permeates the whole of society. In the current New Age, the predominant influences on today's society — technology, materialism, and economic growth — are being rejected in favor of something more sustainable and rooted in deeper and more lasting spiritual values.

The spirit of the ancients

To the modern mind, the ancient civilizations' use of ritual to harness the forces of nature may seem simply superstitious; similarly, those peoples who worship mountains or trees have often been described as primitive. In reality, they were simply affirming the powerful energies contained in these natural objects, and aware of human connectedness to them. The same goes for traditional magicians and sorcerers: they can be seen as technicians working with the laws of the universe rather than those of Western science.

In the New Age, an awareness of these laws and energies has entered our consciousness once again. Their relevance is increasingly acknowledged by conventional science. Many scientific discoveries of the twentieth century – the concept of relativity, chaos theory, the possible existence of parallel universes – were predicted by shamen and Buddhist scholars thousands of years ago. One of the principles of divination, for example. is that significant patterns of energy are reflected in smaller events, such as the falling of a stick. Some branches of physics now describe reality in these very terms.

History teaches us that modern societies are civilized, and that the further back in time one goes, the more primitive, brutish, and uncivilized human life becomes. This prejudice stems largely from nineteenth-century evolutionary theory, and is now being superseded by the realization that many ancient civilizations had profound and highly-developed spiritual and philosophical systems. Perhaps more

MAMA KILYA
Here the Incan Moon goddess gazes upon her own image. Mythology tells of how Mama Kilya threw ashes into her face in order to outshine the her husband and brother the Sun.

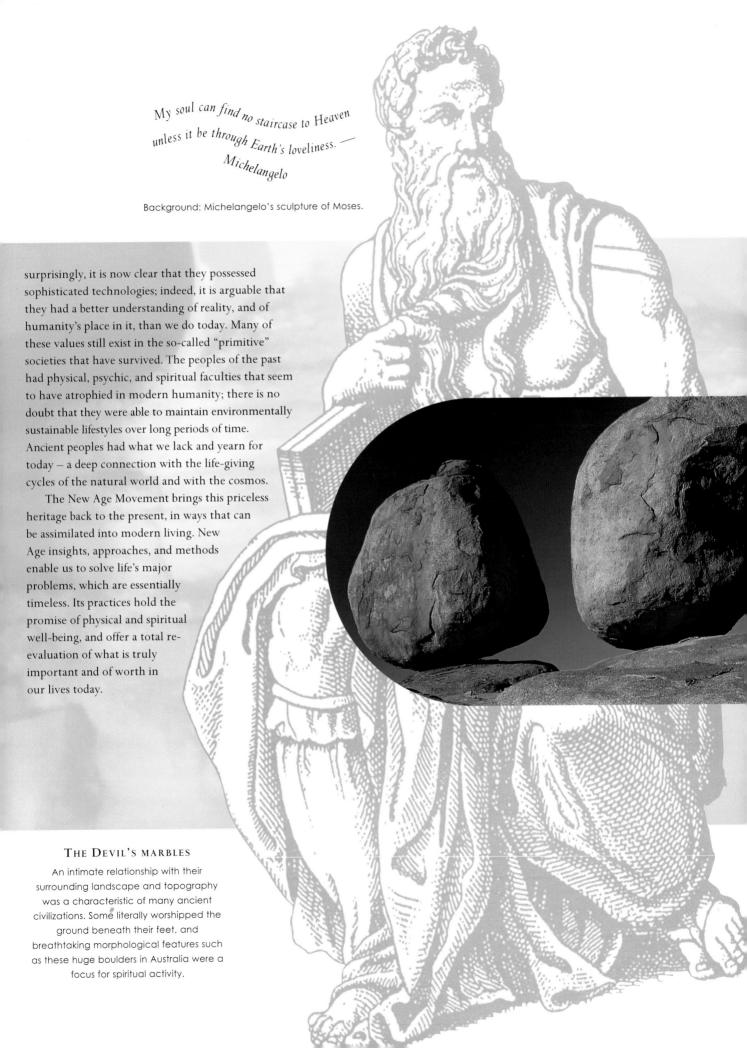

My soul can find no staircase to Heaven unless it be through Earth's loveliness. — Michelangelo

Background: Michelangelo's sculpture of Moses.

surprisingly, it is now clear that they possessed sophisticated technologies; indeed, it is arguable that they had a better understanding of reality, and of humanity's place in it, than we do today. Many of these values still exist in the so-called "primitive" societies that have survived. The peoples of the past had physical, psychic, and spiritual faculties that seem to have atrophied in modern humanity; there is no doubt that they were able to maintain environmentally sustainable lifestyles over long periods of time. Ancient peoples had what we lack and yearn for today — a deep connection with the life-giving cycles of the natural world and with the cosmos.

The New Age Movement brings this priceless heritage back to the present, in ways that can be assimilated into modern living. New Age insights, approaches, and methods enable us to solve life's major problems, which are essentially timeless. Its practices hold the promise of physical and spiritual well-being, and offer a total re-evaluation of what is truly important and of worth in our lives today.

THE DEVIL'S MARBLES

An intimate relationship with their surrounding landscape and topography was a characteristic of many ancient civilizations. Some literally worshipped the ground beneath their feet, and breathtaking morphological features such as these huge boulders in Australia were a focus for spiritual activity.

TIME LINE

10,500 B.C.
The last age of Aquarius and time of the construction of the Sphinx at Giza.

5000 B.C.
Newgrange tomb built in Ireland, designed to harness light during winter solstice, shows proof of early attempts to record the passing of time.

3000 B.C.
Earliest construction of Stonehenge, England.

3000 B.C.
Construction of stone circle at Callanish, Scotland.

1300s B.C.
Construction of Hovenweep Castle, Utah, USA. Site used as an ancient observatory.

1400 B.C.
Chinese record solar eclipses.

1800 B.C.
Babylonians make first astronomical recordings.

500 B.C.
Greeks put forward a model for a solar calendar and identify solstice and equinox points.

0 B.C.
The Earth moves into the constellation of Pisces. Christ is born. Building of the medicine wheel at Moose Mountain, Saskatchewan, Canada.

1–650 A.D.
The Nazca lines are carved into the Peruvian landscape.

1543
Copernicus publishes *De Revolutionius* – its rejection of geocentricism contributes to the decline of astrology.

1600s
Spanish historian Guaman Poma records that four pillars overlooking the Cusco valley, Peru, act as an agricultural calendar. Farmers plant crops according to the alignments between the sun and pillars.

1700s
Scientists creates a backlash against traditional spiritualties. The Royal Society in England declares astrology "a disgrace to reason."

1970
Otter Zell founds a movement devoted to Gaia, after a vision in which he sees the Earth as a living organism evolved from a single cell.

1990s
The Internet becomes the most democratic medium for spreading information about New Age disciplines.

1994
Marlborough Downs, England: a crop circle in the shape of an astrological seal is cut into the landscape. Increasing numbers of crop formations appear every year in this region of England.

2010 AD
The Earth moves into the constellation of Aquarius, and the New Age begins.

The Cosmos and the New Age

This book examines how the New Age Movement has evolved from a rich tapestry of past traditions. A number of characteristics of these civilizations, all of them key to the development of New Age culture and techniques, recur time and again. Chief among them are man's recognition of an intangible spiritual realm alongside the everyday world, and an awareness of his relationship to the cosmos about him. This is most clearly demonstrated in our forefathers' keen interests in the movements of the stars. The widespread discovery of archaeoastronomical sites, some of which are featured on this map, shows that not only was sky-gazing a practical activity that guided sailors across the

KEY

These icons identify a selection of ancient cultural traditions with a close dependence on astronomical patterns.

 Ancient megaliths

 Mursi tribal lands

 Polynesian territories

 Birthplace of Christianity

 Ancient observatories

 Egyptian pyramids

 Records of Dog Star constellation

 Lakota homelands

 Ancient Sun worshippers

 Home of Islam

Home of Chinese philosophy

"As above so below"
As the sun moved counterclockwise through the constellations of the zodiac, the Lakota tribe mirrored this trajectory, moving from one ceremonial site to another, each corresponding to a constellation.

Dog Star
Pre-Columbian rock drawings found at Santa Fe, New Mexico, depict the Dog Star (Sirius) constellation.

Stonehenge, England
On the summer solstice, the heel stone of this stone circle aligns with the sunrise, illustrating Druidic sun worship and early attempts to predict lunar and eclipses and equinoxes.

The Sun Watchers
The Sun priest, or Pekwin, was the most highly regarded member of the Zuni community. His responsibilities included observation of the Sun in order to choose the most propitious time to hold rituals and ceremonies.

Ancient Observatory
A pre-Inca stone circle, built near Lake Titicaca in Bolivia, is believed to have been a sacred observatory used by priests of the cult of a sun-god.

Holy Star
The New Testament tells of a star that led three wise men and shepherds to a stable in Bethlehem to pay homage to the Messiah, whose birth coincides with the start of the current age of Pisces.

Sowing Time
In Ethiopia the Mursi tribe keep track of the four stars in the Southern Cross constellation to find the correct time to plant sorghum and maize.

Map labels

ARCTIC OCEAN

NORTH AMERICA

ATLANTIC OCEAN

PACIFIC OCEAN

SOUTH AMERICA

EUROPE

AFRICA

MOSCOW
Callanish
Newgrange
LONDON
Stonehenge
BERLIN
PARIS
MADRID
ROME
ATHENS
CAIRO
Bethlehem

Moose Mtn.
Montreal
New York
WASHINGTON DC
San Francisco
Black Mtn.
Hovenweep Castle
NEW MEXICO
MEXICO CITY
CARACAS

Lima
Cuzco Valley
Nazca Delta
Lake Titicaca
Rio de Janeiro
BUENOS AIRES

ETHIOPIA
Omo
Cape Town

N

seas and showed farmers the right time to plant crops, but that it underlined man and woman's connection with the universe, and that the earth was a microcosm of a larger cosmos.

In our modern world we still build observatories to watch the stars in order to find out what they can tell us about our past and future. What has changed is the way we look: now we look at the sky scientifically, rather than intuitively or for spiritual understanding. We seem to have lost the ability to see the outer limits of the universe as an extension of our immediate environment. The challenge for the New Age is to regain this sense of interconnectedness and to recognise that when we touch a leaf we disturb a star.

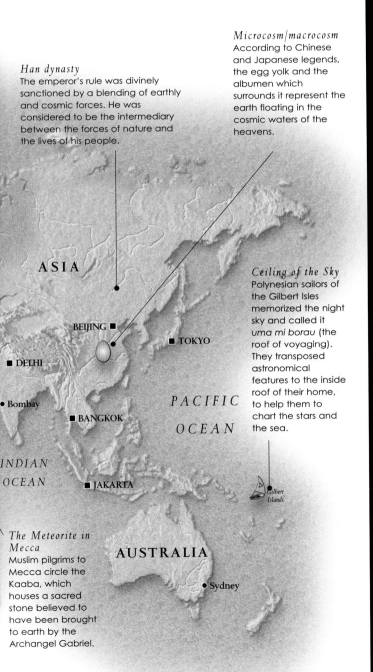

Han dynasty
The emperor's rule was divinely sanctioned by a blending of earthly and cosmic forces. He was considered to be the intermediary between the forces of nature and the lives of his people.

Microcosm/macrocosm
According to Chinese and Japanese legends, the egg yolk and the albumen which surrounds it represent the earth floating in the cosmic waters of the heavens.

Ceiling of the Sky
Polynesian sailors of the Gilbert Isles memorized the night sky and called it *uma mi borau* (the roof of voyaging). They transposed astronomical features to the inside roof of their home, to help them to chart the stars and the sea.

The Meteorite in Mecca
Muslim pilgrims to Mecca circle the Kaaba, which houses a sacred stone believed to have been brought to earth by the Archangel Gabriel.

The Celestial Nile

Theories and speculation ranging from the mundane to the bizarre have been put forward to explain the purpose of the pyramids at Giza. Were they simply intended as tombs for the pharaohs, or would they eventually, as Edgar Cayce – America's "sleeping prophet" – predicted, reveal the mythological "house of records" left by the citizens of Atlantis when they supposedly settled in Egypt?

One theory that has attracted the approval of serious Egyptologists is the alignment of the pyramids with the three stars of Orion's belt. In 1984, in his book *The Orion Mystery*, Robert Bauval suggested that the pattern formed by Orion's belt, and the great hunter's position alongside the Milky Way, would have exactly mirrored that of the three pyramids and their proximity to the Nile in the year 2500 B.C., when it is believed the Sphinx was built. Facing East, and in precise alignment with the equinoxes, the Sphinx has long been regarded as the marker of an age. Of which age no one was sure, as the vernal point above the Sphinx would have been in the constellation of Taurus in 2500 B.C., which raises the question why the monument depicts the body of a lion, rather than a bull. The Egyptologist John Anthony West has confirmed that erosion and weathering on the Sphinx indicates it was built much earlier than previously believed, around 10,500 B.C. Computer simulation has made it possible to recreate accurate maps of the ancient heavens, and these show that the vernal point above the Sphinx at that time would indeed have been in the constellation of Leo.

The ancient Egyptians' cosmological view of themselves makes our recent exploration of the solar system, and our understanding of our place within it, seem rather humble and unimaginative by comparison.

ARCHAEOASTRONOMY IN 10,500 B.C.

At sunrise on the vernal equinox, the pyramids and sphinx combined to form an architectural representation of the Orion constellation. This will happen again in 2010 A.D.

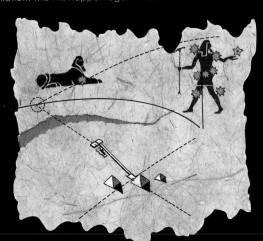

THE AMERICAS

The land masses of North, South, and Central America contain a rich array of spiritual traditions that stretch back to the Pleistocene epoch, before the end of the last Ice Age, during which the first human migrations to the continent occurred. Some of these traditions have lasted into modern times and are often termed "Indian," from the belief prevalent at the time of Columbus that the Americas were the outer reaches of the East Indies. These cultures display rich examples of shamanism, the earliest belief system known to humanity. In their belief in ritual, close communion with, and respect for nature, they have provided much inspiration for the New Age Movement today.

North America

This map shows the origins and key migrations of the main native peoples of North America. Before European settlement, each region supported hundreds of tribes, whose culture evolved with the movement of peoples, tribal wars, and the utilization of the host landscape.

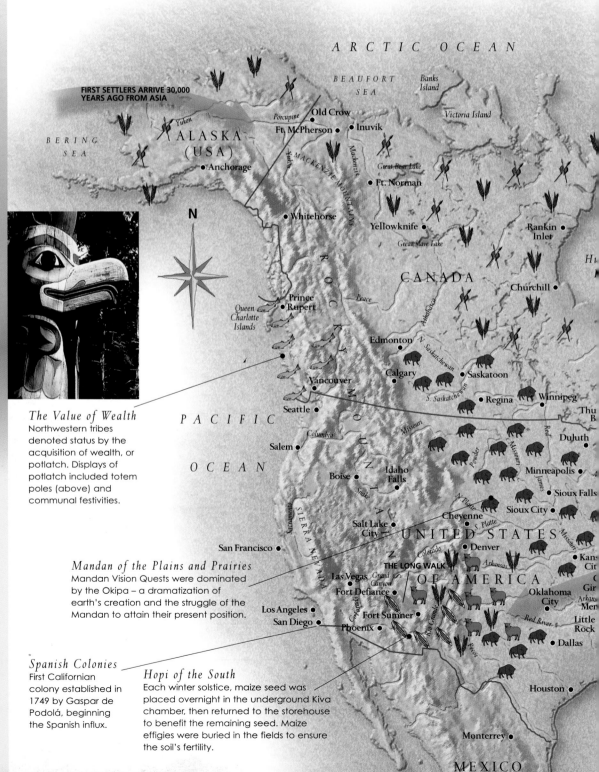

The Value of Wealth
Northwestern tribes denoted status by the acquisition of wealth, or potlatch. Displays of potlatch included totem poles (above) and communal festivities.

Mandan of the Plains and Prairies
Mandan Vision Quests were dominated by the Okipa – a dramatization of earth's creation and the struggle of the Mandan to attain their present position.

Spanish Colonies
First Californian colony established in 1749 by Gaspar de Podolá, beginning the Spanish influx.

Hopi of the South
Each winter solstice, maize seed was placed overnight in the underground Kiva chamber, then returned to the storehouse to benefit the remaining seed. Maize effigies were buried in the fields to ensure the soil's fertility.

KEY

Medicine Culture of the Northeast

Eastern peoples, such as the Mohawk, Seneca, Cayuga, and Onondaga, treated disease by manipulating the spirit world. Medicine men dressed as totem animals and performed the False Face ceremony, in order to harness the power of the chosen animal. As woodland tribes, their masks were carved from local forest bark, highlighting the link between the environment and cultural traditions.

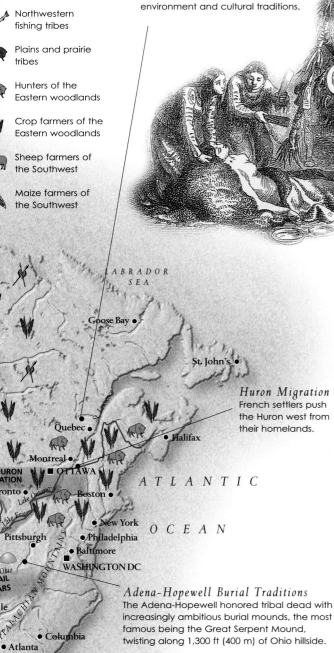

LABRADOR SEA

Goose Bay ●

St. John's ●

Huron Migration

French settlers push the Huron west from their homelands.

Quebec ●

● Halifax

Montreal ●

E HURON
GRATION
■ OTTAWA

Toronto ●
Lake Ontario
● Boston

oit
Lake Erie

● New York

Pittsburgh ●
● Philadelphia

at
ent
ınd
Ohio
● Baltimore
■ WASHINGTON DC

TRAIL
TEARS

ATLANTIC

OCEAN

Adena-Hopewell Burial Traditions

The Adena-Hopewell honored tribal dead with increasingly ambitious burial mounds, the most famous being the Great Serpent Mound, twisting along 1,300 ft (400 m) of Ohio hillside.

ville

● Columbia

● Atlanta

● Jacksonville

● Miami

The early peoples of North America practiced a wide range of cultures and had a highly evolved social system. Some were primarily hunters and gatherers, others were farmers, and others known mainly as warriors. Native tribes claim their culture dates from 160,000 years before written history began.

When white settlers arrived, there were said to be over six hundred ethnic groups, each with distinctive characteristics. European settlement wiped out this diversity and richness of tradition. Cultural traditions were influenced by the physical environment, but there was a broad basis of common spirituality, which has strongly influenced the New Age.

Tribal Locations

The northern hunting and farming tribes included the Algonquin, Inuit, Eskimo, Cree, Ingulik, and Yellow-knife, with the Tlingit, Haida, and Nookta representing the northwest Pacific communities. Coastal tribes hunted fish, sea and land mammals, while inland communities grew cereal crops. Physical dependence on the land inspired the spiritual lore, with salmon-fishing communities deifying the salmon, while woodland tribes carved their totem poles from coniferous trees.

The hunting tribes of the plains and prairies included the Apache, Lakota, Cheyenne, Blackfoot, Arapaho, Comanche, Mandan, Crow, Pawnee, Sioux, Ojibwa, and Hidatsa. They lived in the great open spaces, and so their mythology focused on their hunt animals, such as bison and buffalo.

Hunting and farming communities of the east included the Cherokee, Mohawk, Cayuga, Onondaga, Seneca, and Huron. Spiritual significance was given to maize, beans, and squash, which were named the Three Sisters.

Southern tribes, such as the Hopi, Navajo, Apache, and Zuni, developed a highly sophisticated mythology and global world view. This included predictions about the future of humanity that are increasingly influential today.

Mother Earth, Father Sky

Despite the cultural diversity of the native North American peoples, they all viewed the earth as a sacred mother figure, and the sky as a father.

SOURCE OF ENERGY

The sun was a key deity for most tribes, and their relationship with it was affirmed all over North America during the summer solstice. The Sun Dance, in which the sun was represented by sacred fire, required participants to enter altered states of consciousness through prolonged physical exertion, obtaining mystical visions and awareness of the Great Spirit.

For Native Americans, life was, and still is, based on the primary relationship between people and the natural world. This tradition of respect has been a major inspiration to New Age ecology. Every aspect of creation was interconnected, and every item was considered sacred. So for individuals to improve their lives, whether in relation to hunting, survival, good fortune, health and long life, happiness, or fulfilment, they had to carry out all their actions with a full awareness of their place on earth. This responsibility applied to humans just as it did to everything else; humans were not regarded as dominant or superior, as they were in the world view of the incoming settlers, and still are by the dominant modern European culture.

Sacred Powers

All the supernatural beings within the spiritual world of the American peoples held a sacred status, and communicated through the messenger figures within each community, which could be animate or inanimate. As vital forces in everyday life, the leading spiritual elements were the sun and sky – attributed with male characteristics – and the earth, which was wholly female. All the tribes included creator figures such as Mother Earth, Father Sky, Grandfather Sun, and Grandmother Moon, along with the originator of all things, known as the Great Spirit.

Spiritual Lifestyle

Native communities believed in the importance of collectively living the "right" way, observing ritual, and following a sacred path in life. Individuals were expected to undergo a learning process in which each one developed particular qualities and abilities, and found a unique role in life.

In this cosmology, the world of spirit was not seen as distinct from everyday physical reality. It, too, was totally integrated. The spirits of ancestors were believed to be ever present, and able to give protection and guidance. Correspondingly, appreciation and gratitude for this spiritual support was a key feature of the Native American view of life.

Similar wisdoms: Sun worship was common in many agrarian societies, as it was a key factor in the success of crops. It had great prominence in ancient Egypt, where its daily journey was a feature of communal worship. Ra, the most famous sun-god, also held the title of the first king of Egypt and pharaoh's father. A later Egyptian sun deity, Aton, held supremacy over all other gods during the only monotheistic period in ancient Egypt.

TIMELESS BACKDROP

Moon worship was particularly prominent among the native tribes of the Southwest. The striking desert landscape could only enhance the appearance of a clear night sky and intensify the spiritual power of the Grandmother Moon symbol.

The First People

Many tribes had a creation mythology telling of the marriage between Earth and Sky, which led to the conception of Life. Divine entities such as Sun, Moon, Wind, and Fire acted as intermediaries between humanity and the spirit world, and mythology played a crucial part in determining man's place in the order of things. The Hopi communities of the southwestern United States provide a clear example of how complete rural dependence demanded a natural world view.

Native American mythology, in contrast to Christian creation mythology, did not involve original sin or a fall from grace. The Creator Spirit was not distanced from his creation. Instead, his energy pervaded everything in it, including humanity. This was crucial to the Native American world view, in which the role of humanity was to preserve the natural order, and is in keeping with New Age thought.

The Hopi Nation

The Hopi people regarded themselves as the "first people" of North America. They believed that they had been placed on the Earth to take care of the land through their ceremonial duties, which kept the world in balance. They believed that if the Hopi nation were to vanish, the motion of the earth spinning on its axis would become unstable, water would swallow the land, and many people would perish. There were many other ancient Hopi prophecies regarding the present and future of humanity.

As sedentary farmers, the Hopi subsisted on maize, beans, squash, wheat, and cotton; they killed rabbits and herded sheep. Their spiritual life was maintained by visits of the kachinas, elaborately costumed male tribe-members, who performed ceremonies to encourage the spring rains and sustain tribal well-being.

Hopi Mythology

A Hopi creation legend tells how the first people on Turtle Island cut out a disk of buckskin, tied it to a wooden frame, and flung it into the sky. They sang to it until it settled on the horizon. It shone, but its light was cold. This was how the moon was created. Then they tried again. They cut out another disk, painted it with egg yolks and yellow pollen, gave it a face, and tied corn silk around it. Then they sent this spinning into the sky, where it began to shine brightly and cast warmth over the earth. This was how the sun was born. After this, the Hopi peoples were able to begin their migrations, with the sun, moon, and stars as their guides. They took their maize with them, and when they came to a place where maize would not grow they knew they had come to the limit of their wanderings, and had to turn back.

UNIQUE SETTLEMENTS
The Hopi occupied several villages, built on mesas or steep-sided hilltops, in northeast Arizona. Their multi-storied buildings were usually constructed of stone and roofed with wood, grasses, or reeds, and served as both living quarters and communal meeting places. Mud was used to plaster the walls inside and out, and ladders were used to reach the floors above ground level.

Lakota Eagle song

"I say I was the first one created
I fly higher than the whole of creation
I am the Spotted Eagle
I am the messenger of your Grandfather,
The Great Spirit.
The Spotted Eagle comes in that way;
The Spotted Eagle will speak when he comes."

MUSICAL HERITAGE
This traditional song embodies the Lakota Sioux creation mythology. Chanting it connects the modern individual with the spirit of the Eagle and the highest creative energy of the cosmos.

The magic of medicine

"Medicine" was crucial to tribal spirituality. It represented the life force that exists in everything. There were different types of medicine: plant, animal, and the medicine of inanimate objects. It was mainly administered by the medicine men, whose knowledge of the traditional ceremonies was handed down through the generations.

The concept of medicine was akin to the concepts of vital energy or life force that exist in other cultures, as *ch'i* in China, and *prana* in the Indian subcontinent.

Active and practiced medicine was incorporated into every aspect of Native American life. It played a central part in specialized rituals on key dates of the year, was used to plan important events, including travel or relocation, and to commune with the spirits linked in sickness. Each tribe member would go about his or her daily affairs aware of the power of medicine with which he or she was interacting.

Animal Medicine

As well as being sources of food, animals had special medicinal powers and could relate to humans as teachers, protective spirits, and holders of collective power or totems. They could act as allies, with each animal having qualities specific and suitable for different occasions. The ability of animals to help humans stemmed from the integral kinship between humans and animals in ancient

ANIMAL MAGIC

Different animal species had specific traits that were widely accepted by Native American tribes. Both the individual and the tribal medicine men aimed to harness these qualities to help solve particular problems:

Deer: gentleness
Buffalo: plenty
Raven: knowledge of magic
Lynx: insight into secrets
Rabbit: fear, fertility
Dog: loyalty, support and the ability to sense negative influences
Horse: power, swiftness, and the ability to respond to a sudden challenge or crisis

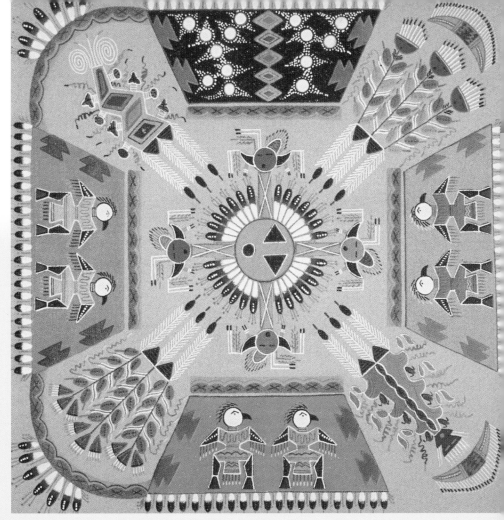

THE IMPORTANCE OF DREAMS

Long before the studies of Carl Jung, Native Americans interpreted their dreams as signs of inner well-being. Dream catchers were symbolic nets used to harness the positive energies of dreams and act as talismans.

times. As New Age followers feel the need to reconnect with the animal world, they may choose to identify with the energies of a particular animal, and hold it as a totem to help steer them through life's difficulties and challenges.

Medicine Objects

Medicine objects were used in ceremony and ritual to express the spirituality of matter. Humans could call upon their powers for help and guidance. They were usually made from the birds and animals that possessed the appropriate medicine.

Far more than decoration, feathers were the most common item used in medicinal ritual. Some tribes kept tethered birds of prey, so that feathers were available when needed for specific ceremonies. Simple prayer feathers found during an individual's Vision Quest initiation journey were also used for ritual purposes. Feathers were inserted into the ground so that their associated prayer could take root and become a reality.

Another use for feathers was to influence dreams. Feathers bound in red thread were hung over a sleeping area or attached to dream catchers, which caught positive dreams and retained their influence in the dreamer's waking life.

A more elaborate medicine object was the prayer arrow, widely used by southern tribes. The arrow was a stick bound in colored threads and feathers. A prayer was formed while the arrow was created, then it was left for the wind to carry the prayer to the Great Spirit.

Medicine objects were used with reverence for the benefits requested and received. Extra offerings were made to the earth, usually something of value to the tribe, such as maize or animal bones.

SAND PAINTINGS

Navajo healers created shamanic sand paintings for traditional "curing ceremonies," and these are still made and used today. The paintings are large circular or square constructions, made with sand that has been colored with natural dyes. There is a different design for each type of illness, and all are committed to memory by the healers. Sand paintings show stylized representations of Navajo spirits, including images of animals, maize, sun, and sky. The person to be healed sits in the center of the painting and absorbs the natural orders of the images, while the illness leaves the body and passes into the painting. These sand paintings have become a very much sought-after New Age art form.

IMBUED WITH MEDICINE POWER

Wooden medicine sticks played a vital role in religious ceremonies. Animal images were often carved into the end of the stick, while feathers and bells added ritualistic power. The talking stick (the shorter of the two shown) was a variation on the medicine stick, intended to impart wisdom and insight to the bearer.

Smudging

Smudging was a traditional Native American technique for purifying and clearing negative energies from individual human auras, from homes or other spaces, and from ritual objects. A mixture of herbs was burned in a large shell, then the smoke was wafted over the person or space with a twig or feather fan. Desert sage was considered to be the most powerful herb for clearing negative vibrations. Cedar or sweetgrass were often added to create positive energy and optimism.

In the wake of the worldwide rediscovery and adoption of Feng Shui and Space Clearing, smudging has once again become a widespread practice. Real estate agents often call in smudging practitioners to clear negative energies in properties that have proved difficult to sell, often with dramatic and immediate results.

Similar wisdoms: Burning herbs or spices to clear negative energies and promote positive spirituality exists in many cultures. In Britain, rosemary was burned on Beltane, the Celtic cross-quarter day, to banish the negative energies that gathered during winter. The ritual continued after the ancient religion was superseded by Christianity, taking place on May Day. Continuing past traditions, the Christian Church introduced incense burning into public worship in the sixth century.

RITUAL ITEMS
The smudging kit consisted of a shell bowl, in which charcoal and selected herbs were burned together to release the aroma, smoke, and essential energies: sage and frankincense were used for purification, and sweetgrass was employed for positivity.

Conquered wilderness

Although the Vision Quest was primarily an individual experience, adult initiation also took the form of group experiences, hunting challenges, and conquest of other tribal lands.

Vision Quests

Native American males traditionally embarked on a Vision Quest as an initiation into maturity, or as a means of finding guidance. Beforehand, they experienced an elaborate process of personal preparation, involving fasting, using a sweat lodge, and other purification methods. Then the individual ventured into the wilderness, taking a blanket but no food or water. The quest would last several days, during which the individual would face up to fears and clarify personal vision in total isolation.

The Vision Quest was a life-changing experience. It enabled the questor to side-step distractions, to regain a more profound perspective on life, and to become more at one with his true self and with the Great Spirit. The power of this practice is being discovered by many New Age seekers for much the same purposes today.

Similar wisdoms: Using a sweat lodge as preparation for a spiritual quest or to bring about feelings of well-being has counterparts in other cultures. They include:

- Ancient Celtic sweat houses, traditionally located near springs
- Traditional Scandinavian and Russian saunas
- Classical Roman baths, and their modern-day equivalents
- Japanese and African steam purification

The Medicine Wheel

The Medicine Wheel was a symbolic representation of the wheel of life, and was used widely among Native Americans for both practical and spiritual purposes. There were minor variations in its use between tribal groups, but its basic meaning was common to all. It is now widely used once more in New Age culture in the search for spiritual harmony.

According to the native fathers, every inch of the earth was sacred and connected to a living creature. As a result, space demanded respect and ceremonial devotion. The Medicine Wheel was an expression of this relationship with space, nature, and the sacred link between the earth and the life and spirit forms who occupied its space.

Chants and dances evolved around the wheel as a means to harmonize the natural cycle of events, known as the Circle of Power or Sacred Hoop of Life. It also aimed to please the spirit world and gather the energies of humans and animals.

Building the Wheel

The Medicine Wheel could take many forms. It could be a huge permanent construction made with stones; a smaller, temporary construction where a tribe set up camp; or a graphically inscribed pattern made on an object, such as a drum. The basic form was a circle with radial spokes, with the four largest stones sited at the cardinal points of the compass. The south stone was placed first, said to be the place of the child. This was followed by the west stone, then the north, and finally the east.

The radial spokes marked out three segments between each point of the compass, making twelve segments in all. It was aligned east to west, according to the position of the sun on the horizon at sunrise and sunset. Each segment had significance, offering a sophisticated analysis of human nature, which in turn could be put to practical use.

Taking the Earthwalk

The Earthwalk was a physical and spiritual route taken around the wheel, so that all segments were covered, and their symbolism experienced. The walk was based on the understanding that each person must stand on every spoke of the wheel of life, and understand its meaning. Following the Earthwalk from south to north, then east to west, took the individual through the experience of death (the Good Red Road) into the world of the grandfathers and grandmothers (the Blue or Black Road).

THE WHEEL AS LUNAR CALENDAR

As the seasons had such a strong resonance in the life cycle, the Medicine Wheel evolved 12 sections linked to the lunar months. Each segment had its own plant or tree spirit, color, mineral, and totem animal, and individuals could identify their animal according to their birth date. The choice of animals varied between tribes.

The four segments represented the progress of the seasons between the solstices and equinoxes, each with their own animal:

East: March 22 – June 21: The eagle, standing for peace.

South: June 22 – September 21: The buffalo, standing for warmth.

West: September 22 – December 21: The bear, standing for rain and fertility.

North: December 22 – March 21: The wolf, standing for cold weather and wind.

NO LIMITS

In the vast landscape of the tribal territory, there was no limit to the size of the wheel: this semi-permanent structure uses large rocks as pointers.

The north/south axis symbolized the relationship between heaven and earth, while the east/west axis represented the concept of living within time.

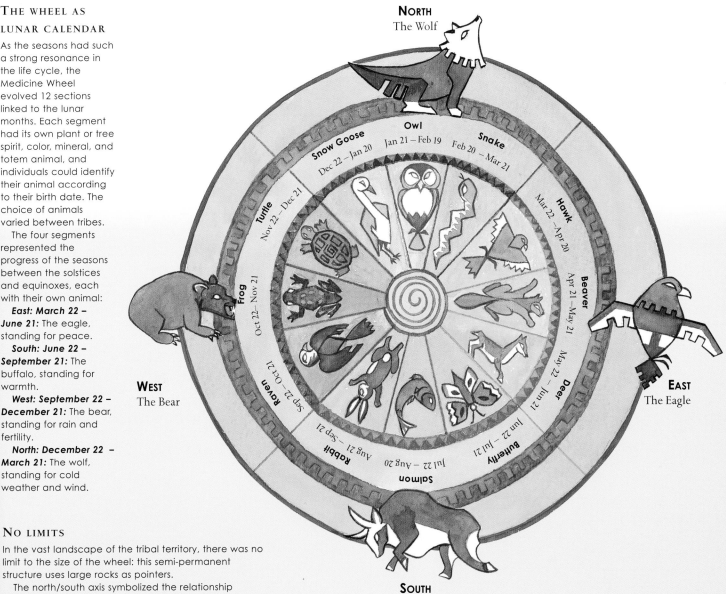

NORTH
The Wolf

EAST
The Eagle

WEST
The Bear

SOUTH
The Buffalo

Snow Goose
Dec 22 – Jan 20

Owl
Jan 21 – Feb 19

Snake
Feb 20 – Mar 21

Hawk
Mar 22 – Apr 20

Beaver
Apr 21 – May 21

Deer
May 22 – Jun 21

Butterfly
Jun 22 – Jul 21

Salmon
Jul 22 – Aug 20

Rabbit
Aug 21 – Sep 21

Raven
Sep 22 – Oct 21

Frog
Oct 22 – Nov 21

Turtle
Nov 22 – Dec 21

Walking the Medicine Way

You can experience animal medicine first hand with a pack of medicine cards. The cards are a recent development, created to harness the teachings of animal medicine in a convenient format. They provide a modern method of balancing one's mind, body, and spirit using the power of this ancient heritage.

Calling on Nature's Power

Animals, as fellow creatures, were said to relay healing powers to anyone who could learn from their life pattern and sense of inner peace. Healing was not only necessary for the individual, but for the ancestors, Earth Mother, and other spirit beings – animals provided access to this medicine.

The Six Elders

In ancient times, when tribe members needed guidance, they would come before the six elders. One elder would motion to the seeker to pull items from his medicine bag, and place them on the ground. These items – a wolf's tooth, a bear's claw, all symbols of individual animals – formed one of the key tenets of Native American medicine. The selection of items and their placement was interpreted by another elder, and used to read the situation, foretell the future, and give guidance to the seeker after wisdom. It is this ceremony that forms the basis of the modern-day medicine cards.

CONSULTING THE ELDERS

The elders consisted of three men and three women. They wore full ceremonial dress and feathered head dress, as they awaited the tribe member seeking guidance.

Understanding Medicine Cards

Medicine cards allow you to be your own "elder," and divine for yourself or a friend with a personalized reading. Each animal has its own qualities, representing the lesson it has to impart to those who seek wholeness. The self-knowledge gained through consulting the cards and following their guidance is said to increase one's personal power.

Finding Your Totem

Each person is said to have nine totem animals that represent their own personal medicine, emulate their talents, and also provide a source of inspiration for self-improvement. Seven of the animals should accompany you on your Earthwalk (see right), and the remaining two will walk on your left and right sides at all times. These remaining totems may come to you in dreams or through a more intuitive process.

For example, the eagle represents spirit and provides a connection with the divine Great Spirit. As eagles soar, they are said to be observant of life's changing patterns. When individuals lack the eagle's qualities, they may have forgotten their link with the Great Spirit and must seek love to help heal their broken wings.

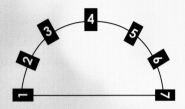

THE EARTHWALK DIRECTIONS

When you embark on life's Earthwalk, there are seven physical directions you can take: **1** East, **2** South, **3** West, **4** North, **5** Above, **6** Below, and **7** Within. Choose a totem animal for each point, the same as, or in addition to, your nine personal totems. The Earthwalk animals offer guidance for living each direction, and are selected by contemplation of the 44 animals.

ONE ANIMAL, ONE TOTEM

The one guiding animal for each individual may be chosen from the Medicine Wheel in relation to birth date, or by personal choice. The wolf is a popular totem animal, as it shows immense loyalty to its mate and pack. Wolf medicine empowers the teacher within us to impart understanding.

The 44 animals and their characteristics

1. Eagle - *spirit*
2. Hawk - *messenger*
3. Elk - *stamina*
4. Deer - *gentleness*
5. Bear - *introspection*
6. Snake - *change*
7. Skunk - *reputation*
8. Otter - *feminine qualities*
9. Butterfly - *transformation*
10. Turtle - *Mother Earth*
11. Moose - *self-esteem*
12. Porcupine - *innocence*
13. Coyote - *trickery*
14. Dog - *loyalty*
15. Wolf - *teacher*
16. Raven - *magic*
17. Mountain lion - *leadership*
18. Lynx - *secrets*
19. Buffalo - *prayer and plenty*
20. Mouse - *scrutiny*
21. Owl - *deception*
22. Beaver - *builder*
23. Opossum - *diversion*
24. Crow - *law*
25. Fox - *camouflage*
26. Squirrel - *gathering*
27. Dragonfly - *illusion*
28. Armadillo - *boundaries*
29. Badger - *aggressiveness*
30. Rabbit - *fear*
31. Turkey - *give away*
32. Ant - *patience*
33. Weasel - *stealth*
34. Grouse - *sacred spiral*
35. Horse - *power*
36. Lizard - *dreams*
37. Antelope - *action*
38. Frog - *cleansing*
39. Swan - *grace*
40. Dolphin - *manna*
41. Whale - *record keeper*
42. Bat - *rebirth*
43. Spider - *weaving*
44. Hummingbird - *joy*

Reading the medicine cards

Medicine cards can be laid out in a variety of ways for different purposes. The cards portray 44 animals, together with a picture, number, and talismans that evoke that creature's particular medicine.

The cards can be used or consulted in a number of ways, according to the individual's needs. A single animal spirit can be adopted as a long-term ally. The creature can be an ongoing source of support, or drawn from the pack for inspiration in times of need.

For a more detailed consultation, some of the cards can be laid out in a special way, then interpreted according to their positions. The overall picture given by the cards will reflect the individual's personality, circumstances, strengths and weaknesses, and will provide insight into his or her situation.

Dealing with reverse cards

When taking the cards from the pack, the animal and its corresponding number may appear the right way up or down. Do not right the cards as you lay them out – leave them upside-down if that is the way they come, as this placement signifies the reverse or contrary of the usual card meaning.

MEDICINE WHEEL LAYOUT

One card is placed in each of the four cardinal compass positions and a fifth card in the center. Each of the four directions reveals one animal, whose meaning and attributes provide direction for personal contemplation and decision making.

North
The card in this position is the key to walking in wisdom and how to apply the lessons of the other cards.

South
The south card tells you what elements you need to trust in yourself, and what you need to nurture for the future.

East
This card reveals where your spiritual strengths lie and the major challenge to seeing your situation clearly.

West
This card gives you the internal solution to your present challenges.

Center
This card is called the Sacred Mountain or Sacred Tree card and indicates your present spiritual state and issues you should tackle today.

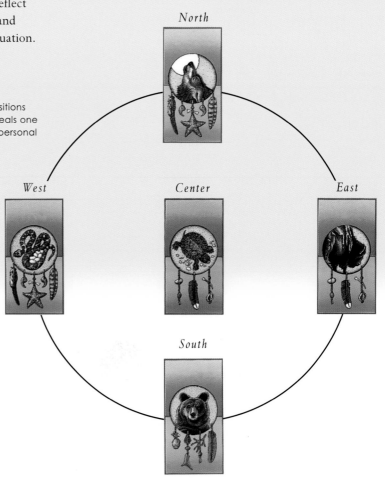

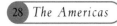

North

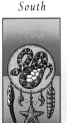

South

East

West

Card 6

Card 4

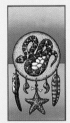

Card 3

Card 2

Card 1

Left   *Right*

Card 5   *Card 7*

BUTTERFLY LAYOUT

As a totem animal, the butterfly represents transformation, and in keeping with its characteristics, this spread is used to determine, guide, and predict the outcome of group enterprises. Four cards are placed in the compass positions, and indicate the stages the given project will move through until conclusion. The language used to read this spread makes vivid reference to the lifecycle of the butterfly – the egg, the larva, and the cocoon.

North
This card is known as the Butterfly card or Butterfly position. It indicates if the Great Spirit has been with your project through its development.

South
This is the Larva card, and is about the early action that must be taken, and which medicine must be used to achieve a pragmatic result, and to shed the negative egos of the individuals involved, just as a caterpillar replenishes its own skin.

East
This is the Egg card, and should be viewed as the nucleus or seed of the project. Allow the medicine of the animal card to give value to the inner core of the plan.

West
This is the Cocoon card and speaks of higher purpose. It is where ultimate transformation takes place, as found inside the cocoon of a butterfly. On viewing, you should ask yourself the reasons behind the project undertaken – if it is purely self-serving, it is likely to fail.

MOTHER EARTH, FATHER SKY LAYOUT

This spread is used for balancing your male and female sides in times of confusion. The male side, symbolized by Father Sky, contains warrior energy, courage, and medicine powers. The female side, seen through Mother Earth, is the intuitive side of the mind, with nurturing, creative forces.

Left
This is the Mother Earth card and you should use the medicine of the particular animal to help restore your female attributes: creativity, wisdom, and goddess energy.

Right
The Father Sky card offers an opportunity to confirm your male strengths – ideas and adventure – using the qualities of the animal on the card.

PATHWAY LAYOUT

This layout is a modern arrangement, derived from the ancient Druidic system or Celtic oracle cards of divination, giving you general inspiration about the pathway of your life.

This spread highlights the shift in emphasis for divination tools such as the medicine cards, from a means to analyze the present and predict the future, to a New Age, where the emphasis is on gaining insight into one's personal qualities and situation in order to maximize one's potential.

Card 1
This animal on this card indicates your past spiritual position.

Card 2
This animal indicates your present spiritual position.

Card 3
This animal indicates your future spiritual position.

Card 4
This animal indicates the set of life lessons you are experiencing currently.

Card 5
This animal indicates the challenge you have just conquered.

Card 6
This animal indicates what elements of your life are working for you.

Card 7
This animal indicates what elements of your life are not working at this time.

Spirit Power of the Innua

The Inuit people live in the northernmost extremes of the American continent, along the coast of Canada and Alaska, and also to the west across the sea in adjacent northeastern Siberia and to the east in Greenland. They are closely related to the ancient people of central Asia and Siberia.

Inuit culture is shamanistic, and has been well preserved until relatively recently by the inhospitable nature of the Arctic. To the Inuit people, sometimes inaccurately called "Eskimos," spirit powers, or *Innua*, exist in every natural thing, including animals, fish, plants, water, and rocks. These natural forces, which are akin to the medicine energies held sacred by more southerly tribes, serve as guardians of the people, or "Torngak." Polar bears, for instance, possess especially powerful and sought-after Innua.

The Inuit shaman is known as the "Angakok." At times of trouble, for example when hunting is poor or people have no food, he makes a shamanic journey to encounter the relevant spirits. Since the ocean is the Inuits' greatest source of food, it has a particularly powerful spirit – a fertility figure known as Sedna, the old woman who lives in its depths. She controls its creatures, and also influences the weather above it.

The Inuit have a range of shamanistic divination methods. These are used to seek guidance about matters such as where to hunt, or where to move the settlement.

OCEAN LIVING

Fish and sea mammals traditionally provided the Inuit with food, clothing, oil, tools, and weapons, making them extremely efficient hunters, with a close-tied relationship with the animal world. Although old practices have died out for many communities, their link with the earth and natural environment remains a vital part of the culture, and is a primary source of inspiration for the New Age Movement.

Nanook, the Bear, symbolized primal
strength, altruism and idealism.
Sequinek, the Sun Woman, signified positive
action and the seizing of opportunity.
Aningan, the Moon Man, represented winter
and darkness, and the time for rest.

Major Inuit Divination Methods

- Dreams are considered an important source of information
  about animals and future events. They are also used to help
  with making decisions. The Inuit believe that animal spirits
  use the language of dreams to communicate with humans.
- In drum divination, the surface of the drum is decorated
  with symbols representing animals and other elements. A
  ring is placed on it, and the drum is beaten. When the ring
  comes to rest, a divination is obtained from the symbol
  upon which it has landed.
- In bone divination, the shoulder bone of a reindeer or
  caribou is heated until it cracks. The shaman then
  interprets the pattern made by the cracks.

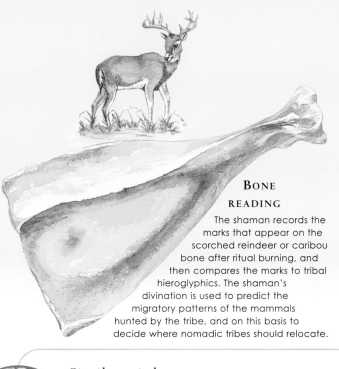

BONE
READING

The shaman records the
marks that appear on the
scorched reindeer or caribou
bone after ritual burning, and
then compares the marks to tribal
hieroglyphics. The shaman's
divination is used to predict the
migratory patterns of the mammals
hunted by the tribe, and on this basis to
decide where nomadic tribes should relocate.

Similar wisdoms: In ancient China,
tortoise shells were used instead of bones
for divination, illustrating the
effect of the local fauna on
native spiritual traditions.
This method formed the origins
of the I Ching.

TIME LINE

32,000–30,000 B.C.
Southeast Asians visit
South America.

30,000–10,000 B.C.
Continent constantly
colonized by migrations.

800 B.C.
Peak of Olmec culture.

400–900 A.D.
Nazca lines formed.

950–1150
Toltecs settle in Tulla.

1200–1325
Aztecs appoint King
Azcapotzalco, forming
link with Toltec nation.

1426
Aztec war with
Maxtlatzin, successor to
Azcapotzalco. Aztecs
follow Tlacaelel dogma
of mystic militarism.

1519
Hernando Cortes lands
in Mexico.

1520
Aztec–Spanish wars.
Montezuma dies in
battle. Aztec culture
destroyed.

1810
Mexican revolt. Priest
Hidalgo Y Costilla issues
the Grito de Dolores
(Cry of Dolores), calling
for racial equality and
land redistribution.

1813
Henequen and sugar
mark the "green gold"
trade boom in Yukatan.

1821
Mexico gains
independence.

1977
Xapui Rural Workers
Union formed, marking
economic confidence
of native workers.

1989
Musician Sting forms the
Rainforest Foundation
to save Brazilian jungle,
raising over $5 million.

1990s
Ancient Colombian
Kogi tribe publicized by
Western media.

2012
The end of the fifth age
of Mayan calendar.

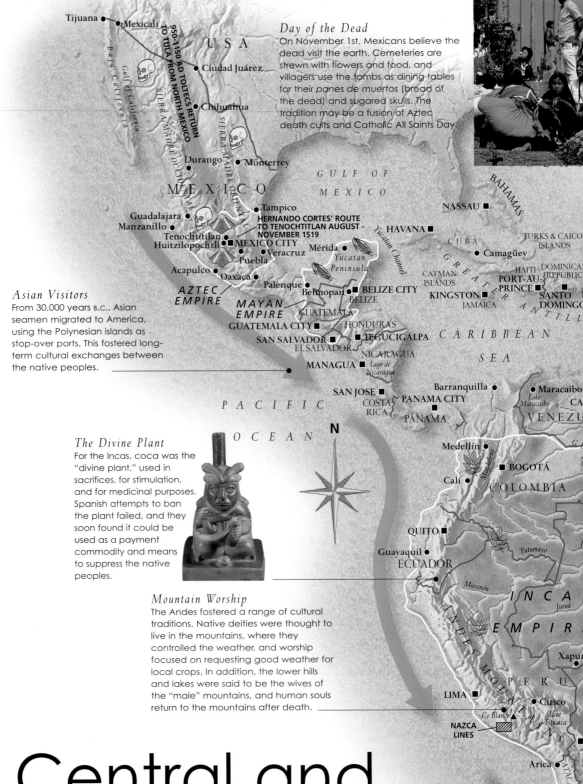

Day of the Dead
On November 1st, Mexicans believe the dead visit the earth. Cemeteries are strewn with flowers and food, and villagers use the tombs as dining tables for their *panes de muertos* (bread of the dead) and sugared skulls. The tradition may be a fusion of Aztec death cults and Catholic All Saints Day.

Asian Visitors
From 30,000 years B.C., Asian seamen migrated to America, using the Polynesian islands as stop-over ports. This fostered long-term cultural exchanges between the native peoples.

The Divine Plant
For the Incas, coca was the "divine plant," used in sacrifices, for stimulation, and for medicinal purposes. Spanish attempts to ban the plant failed, and they soon found it could be used as a payment commodity and means to suppress the native peoples.

Mountain Worship
The Andes fostered a range of cultural traditions. Native deities were thought to live in the mountains, where they controlled the weather, and worship focused on requesting good weather for local crops. In addition, the lower hills and lakes were said to be the wives of the "male" mountains, and human souls return to the mountains after death.

Central and South America

Central and South America produced stunning physical structures with intense cultural meaning. These sites are now a focus for New Age spiritual pilgrimage, and a renaissance in ancient rites.

KEY

This key indicates the main regional groups prior to European settlement.

- Empire boundaries
- Rainforest tribes
- Coca leaf farmers
- Maize farmers
- Major temples and pyramids
- Day of the Dead celebrations

SPANISH AND PORTUGESE COLONIZATION

BARBADOS
ST. VINCENT & THE GRENADINES
GRENADA
TRINIDAD & TOBAGO

The Burning Season
Just before the rainy season, farmers burned the scorched vegetation in their felled tree forests in order to replenish the soil. In modern times, intensive farming and felling methods have destroyed native ecosystems and the physical basis of the rural cultures.

Modern Protesters
Deep in the Brazilian rainforest, Chico Mendes, a local rubber trapper, started campaigning to save the rainforest and prevent excessive felling. He was assassinated for his pains, and his killers have never been caught.

GEORGETOWN
GUYANA
PARAMARIBO
CAYENNE
SURINAM FRENCH GUIANA (FRANCE)
Macapá
Belém
São Luis
Fortaleza
Manaus
Amazon
Madeira
Tapajós
Xingu
Tocantins
BRAZIL
CAMPOS
Araguaia
Parnaíba
CAATINGAS
São Francisco
Recife
Maceió
Arinos
Salvador
Paraná
PLANALTO DE MATO GROSSO
BRAZILIAN HIGHLANDS
BRASÍLIA
BOLIVIA
Belo Horizonte
PARAGUAY
Pilcomayo
São Paulo
Rio de Janeiro
ASUNCIÓN
ATLANTIC OCEAN
Uruguay
Pôrto Alegre
URUGUAY
ARGENTINA
MONTEVIDEO
BUENOS AIRES
Bahia Blanca

Ancient cultures of Central and South America shared common themes with native North Americans. With their interdependence on the rural landscape, they had the same respect for the natural world, and its influence on human life. However, as the Mesoamerican civilizations developed, they abandoned the predominantly nomadic lifestyle of their northern neighbors, and this new sense of settlement was reflected in their spirituality.

Cultural Achievements

Ancient Mesoamerica was home to great building empires, responsible for large, permanent cities and dramatic architecture. They developed sophisticated astronomical and astrological techniques and related systems of divination on which they based their civil and religious life. The passage of time and celestial influences were key themes in their cultural identification. As with North America, these cultures were eventually colonized and assimilated, in this case by the Spanish conquistadors.

RAYMI FESTIVAL

Raymi was the Incan festival to honor the sun god. With a renewed interest in ancient American cultures, this service is now being restaged to keep the native cultural heritage alive.
The Inca Quichua language shows some similarities with the Indian language Sanskrit – the Hindu son of the sun is named Rama.

The Mayan calendar

The Maya occupied the Mexican Yucatan peninsula, Guatemala, and Honduras. With a grasp of mathematics that was far in advance of their time, they developed intricate calendars for civil and ceremonial use. Renewed interest in their scientific achievements has led to a New Age renaissance in their spiritual traditions.

Mac

Pop

Uayeb

Xul

Zotz

Zac

Chen

Pax

Kankin

Uo

Kumku

Yaxkin

Zec

Ceh

Yax

Kayab

Muan

Zip

Moi

Mayan mythology and spiritual traditions were based on the idea that the universe was in a constant state of struggle between life-giving powers such as warmth and fertility, and negative powers such as death and famine.

Calendar Structures

There were two Mayan calendars. The civil calendar, Haab, was a 19-month, 365-day year cycle, recurring in 52-year cycles. The sacred calendar, Tzolkin, was based on 13 months of 20 days each, and one month of five days, with significant 260-day units within the cycle. The Tzolkin calendar was more astronomically accurate than the Western Gregorian equivalent. It was used for personal readings according to birth dates, to time personal events, and for divination.

Mayan Spirituality

Mayan astrology was geared toward spirituality. Their destiny was said to be determined by the Creation Epochs, each lasting 5,125 years. Today, we are living in the Fifth Age, which began in 3114 B.C., and ends at the winter solstice in 2012 A.D. Mayans made accurate predictions about the movements of comets, and their ceremonial buildings were centers for ritual astrology. Their rulers were priest-kings with exclusive access to the scientific and esoteric readings of civil and religious astronomers. Although the religious emphasis of Mayan culture shifted with the influences of other cultures, ritual divination was a continuing theme, based on time-specific celestial predictions.

CORRECTING THE CALENDAR

Above right: this carving from the Mayan altar at Copán, Honduras shows the state astronomers convening to correct the Mayan calendar in 776 B.C. Time-keeping is a constant theme of Mayan culture.
Left: Haab, the civil Mayan calendar, featured 19 months, shown here with their corresponding pictograms.

Similar wisdoms: Asian civilizations also place great importance on linking human destiny to long passages of time. Chinese systems measure varying periods of time from 60 days up to eras of 2,200 and 24,000 years. As with the Mayan calendar, pictograms are used to illustrate the attributes of these units of time.

The African Dogon communities wove their own astrological discoveries into religious practice, believing their ancestors were visited by space travelers.

Pyramids and Patterns

The leading Mesoamerican civilizations – Incan, Mayan, Toltec, and Aztec – served their deities with great pyramids planned according to advanced mathematical principles and finished with intricate stone masonry.

The Mesoamericans' mastery of astronomy, architecture, mathematics, and stone carving reached its pinnacle with their enormous pyramid structures. The pyramids served both as temples and astronomical observatories, and have since been recognized as sources of magnetic energy. The ancient cultures of the Mesoamericans are being rediscovered in modern times, as New Age pilgrims flock to the remaining pyramid sites.

The pyramids have over time displayed curious properties that challenge our current understanding of science. These include the ability to preserve organic matter and sharpen razor blades, as if the form of construction affects the material's inherent energetic properties. X-ray surveys inside in the pyramids have also revealed the existence of contradictory force fields. When this information came to light in the 1960s, Western researchers created model pyramids in order to simulate their properties. Pyramid-shaped crystals are now often used as healing aids.

URBAN COSMOS
The sacred city of Teotihuacan was laid out in imitation of the whole cosmos, with the Toltec pyramid of the Sun (right) being one of the primary ritual locations. The Sun Temple at Cuzco, Peru, shared similar principles, with its structural lines radiating into the countryside.

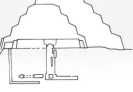

PYRAMID STRUCTURE
Left: The pyramids had a facing of limestone rubble, and were usually ascended by steep stairs.
Above: The interior structure consisted of individual chambers above and below ground, roofed with lime concrete or wooden beams. In contrast to the Aztec structures, Mayan pyramids were noted for their intricate exterior stone carving, rather than their size.

Earth patterns

The Mesoamerican preoccupation with geometric patterns is evident in their fashioning of the local landscape. In the Peruvian desert, there is a great man-made creation that has puzzled observers for centuries – a huge complex of lines marked on the ground. As well as straight lines, there are also spirals, triangles, and enormous representational figures of birds, fish, spiders, and whales. These lines were created by the Nazca civilization between 400 B.C. and 900 A.D., and held a seasonal significance for farming and hunting practices. In a similar way to the pyramids, they also formed a symbolic model of the universe for ritual and devotional use.

Similar wisdoms:

In the Chaco Canyon, New Mexico, the huge curved ruins and straight tracks of the Anazazi nation also display a clear geometric vision, reminiscent of the Nazca lines.

Ancient Nation Rediscovered

Unlike the lost cultures of ancient Central and South America, the Kogi people have remained virtually unchanged in their native Colombian rainforest to the present day.

The Kogi refer to themselves as the Elder Brothers. Their mythology talks of their pyramid-shaped mountain home, known as the Heart of the World, where they guard the land for humankind – the Younger Brothers.

In the 1990s, the Kogi made themselves known to the West, and their spiritual message has had a great impact on New Age consciousness. They descend from an ancient people who inhabited the city of Taironas, renowned for its gold ceremonial objects. They have preserved their traditional way of life for over four hundred years, avoiding any form of contact with the rest of humanity. When outside pollution reached them, they took their message to the world, to stress the importance of preserving the natural environment.

EUROPE

Colonized by successive waves of migration and invasion from east to west, Europe has been ravaged throughout the centuries by many great and destructive wars. At the same time, the ethnic mix we know as European has nourished art and culture of the highest degree, from the classical civilizations of Greece to the Renaissance, and ultimately exported it to the rest of the world in the period of European colonization and emigration. The history of Europe is above all the story of peoples constantly on the move, spreading their spiritual heritage as they went, and it is this that makes it a rich source of inspiration for the New Age Movement.

Bumper Harvests
In 1963 the Findhorn Community created a garden on the barren sand dunes of the Moray Firth, Scotland, which has since become a place of pilgrimage for New Age Christians. Convinced that spiritual communication with the plants is the key to cultivation, the community rejects conventional farming methods.•

Crop Rotation
The 4,000 year-old Callanish stone circle in Scotland was originally built on ancient farming land. The stones became covered in peat, which was itself removed in the 19th century for fuel. The land is now farmed again with arable crops.

Ancient Astronomy
Stonehenge aligns with the morning sunrise on the summer solstice. Neo-pagans and Druids still gather to witness the phenomenon, which is thought to be evidence of ancient sun worship and attempts to predict eclipses and equinoxes.

Europe

Although ancient European culture was rocked by the spread of Christianity, the legacy of the major native groups survives through their stunning megalithic arrangements, and a host of ancient spiritual traditions.

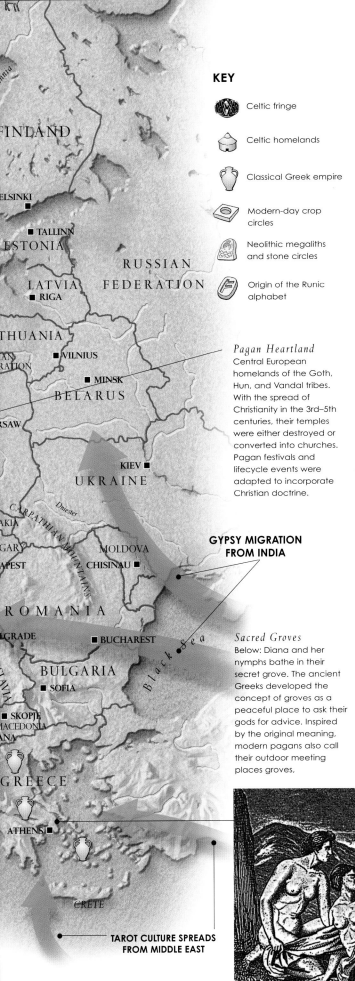

KEY

Celtic fringe

Celtic homelands

Classical Greek empire

Modern-day crop circles

Neolithic megaliths and stone circles

Origin of the Runic alphabet

Pagan Heartland
Central European homelands of the Goth, Hun, and Vandal tribes. With the spread of Christianity in the 3rd–5th centuries, their temples were either destroyed or converted into churches. Pagan festivals and lifecycle events were adapted to incorporate Christian doctrine.

GYPSY MIGRATION FROM INDIA

Sacred Groves
Below: Diana and her nymphs bathe in their secret grove. The ancient Greeks developed the concept of groves as a peaceful place to ask their gods for advice. Inspired by the original meaning, modern pagans also call their outdoor meeting places groves,

TAROT CULTURE SPREADS FROM MIDDLE EAST

The classical empires of Greece and Rome had an immense influence on modern culture. These civilizations built upon very early forms of spirituality, using them to develop their own pagan belief systems, with a pantheon of gods and goddesses, methods of divination, healing, and other practices.

It was an even earlier civilization, however, that seems destined to have the most lasting impact on the New Age Movement. The successive waves of migration by the Celtic tribes, from their original home in Asia Minor all the way across Europe to the Atlantic coasts, brought about an extraordinary flowering of art, culture, and religion in bronze-age Europe. With their ornate decorative artwork and their advanced understanding of astronomy, the Celts also brought a highly evolved religious and spiritual system based on a close understanding of the rhythms of nature. Although subdued militarily by the highly organized armies of the Roman Empire, the Celts and their culture survived in northwest Europe for a further 600 years in relative harmony with the newcomers. It wasn't until the invasions of the Saxons, Angles, and Jutes towards the middle of the first millennium that the Celtic peoples were finally driven to the northern and western fringes of the continent, where they are still to be found today. These areas – Scotland, Ireland, Wales, Cornwall, and Brittany in Northwest France – are today known collectively as the Celtic Fringe.

As well as developing its own belief systems, Europe has also been influenced by adjacent older cultures. The development of the tarot is a good example of this. Although it has become an archetypal divination tool in the West, it was actually profoundly influenced by the esoteric magic of ancient Egypt, the Jewish mystical system known as the cabala, and other archaic sources.

Sacred stones

Standing stones are among the most impressive prehistoric monuments in Europe. The greatest of these are concentrated in Britain and northwestern France, and were built from around 3500 to 1500 B.C.

There are around a thousand stone circles in Britain and over eighty henges (circular structures, often containing stones or wooden posts). In France, particularly in Brittany, there are numerous stone circles and lines and over 1,200 single standing stones. A similar tradition of standing stones can be found in the Pyrenees and in Corsica.

Although the purpose of these monuments can never be known with certainty, it is believed that they were used for shamanic rituals and served as open-air temples. Although the religious beliefs of the builders of these monuments can only be guessed at, astronomical and seasonal events were undoubtedly important, and theories have even been put forward that some of these monuments were highly evolved

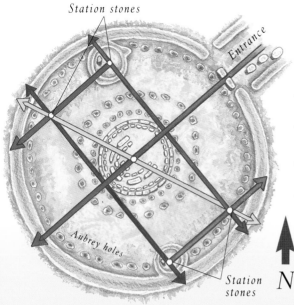

Station stones

Entrance

Aubrey holes

Station stones

N

ASTRONOMICAL ALIGNMENTS

Left: The arrows on this plan of Stonehenge show some of the alignments of the stones: summer solstice sunrise (red); winter solstice sunset (purple); northernmost and southernmost risings of the moon (blue); sunrises and sunsets of equinoxes (yellow). The Aubrey holes may have been used to calculate lunar eclipses.

STONEHENGE AT SUNRISE

Right and below: At summer solstice, the rising sun at dawn is framed by the stones that align with the main entry point through the outer circle. Stonehenge is still one of the most evocative sites in Britain, and New Age believers gather there each year to celebrate Midsummer Day on June 24th.

astronomical observatories. Many of the stones were carefully aligned with the movement of celestial bodies at key points in the year: for example, some were oriented to the position of the sun on the horizon at solstices or equinoxes; others were oriented to significant alignments of the stars, which were believed to affect the well-being of the people, their crops, and animals. In 1974, it was discovered that the fifty-six Aubrey holes at Stonehenge could have been used to predict eclipses.

Modern visitors still claim to feel the power of these constructions, and local folklore often includes traditions about the healing powers of the stones. Today, New Age believers hold these ancient sites in reverence; Stonehenge, for example, is used as a site for summer solstice celebrations.

Sites of Megalithic Monuments

- Stonehenge in Wiltshire, England, is probably the most celebrated ancient monument in the West, and is still used as a center for spiritual practice today.
- The Avebury complex, also in Wiltshire, England, includes a mile-long avenue of standing stones and two massive stone circles. The larger circle consists of almost a hundred stones.
- Callanish stone circle, on the Outer Hebridean isle of Lewis off northwest Scotland, is of modest diameter but contains particularly tall, thin stones.
- Newgrange, in the Boyne Valley in Ireland, includes a large underground chamber, housed in a massive quartz-faced, rounded structure.
- Carnac in Brittany, France, consists of over 2,600 standing stones, out of an estimated original 11,000. They are arranged in parallel lines across miles of French countryside.

Ley Lines

Ley lines are straight lines linking prominent natural and manmade places of sanctity, often corresponding to prehistoric trackways. Many people believe that they follow natural lines of magnetic energy flowing near the surface of the earth, and that ancient civilizations purposely located sacred sites along these lines in order to harness that energy.

It was English naturalist Alfred Watkins who first drew attention to ley lines. When riding in the countryside on a particularly clear day, he stopped at a high point to look at the view. He noticed that many important features of the landscape – such as ancient monuments, burial mounds, stone circles, standing stones, holy wells, churches, and groups of trees – were connected along networks of long, straight lines. Further study of old maps confirmed that this was the case. Watkins' book of 1925, *The Old Straight Track*, in which he expounds this theory, has become a New Age classic.

Ley lines vary in scale and energy level: some cross whole countries; others belong to smaller, local networks. One theory is that the larger networks of lines resulted from the cooling of the earth's surface. Points where leys intersect are believed to be particularly potent.

Crop Circles

Crop circles – spontaneous, intricate patterns of flattened crops in cornfields – are believed by some to be connected to the energies of ancient sites and ley lines. These have occurred mostly in southwest England, where there are many megalithic monuments, but also in other parts of Europe, Australasia, and the Americas. Although many examples are proven hoaxes, others remain unexplained.

CROP CIRCLES

The densest occurrence of crop circles in the world has occurred in southwest England. This area also contains the most powerful ley line crossings, the most significant ancient monuments, and the greatest concentration of alleged UFO sightings in Britain. The white horse in the background is carved into the chalk hillside. Many chalk carvings were produced in southern England by the ancient Celts and Saxons, and the practice witnessed a resurgence in the eighteenth century.

SALISBURY CATHEDRAL

Salisbury Cathedral lies on the ley line that connects Stonehenge with a number of other important sites in Britain. Significant power places on ley lines have long been tapped into for spiritual energies, and churches and cathedrals were often built on sites previously used for Neolithic, Celtic, and Anglo-Saxon spiritual and shamanistic purposes. The inherent energies of these locations are increasingly being recognized in the New Age.

SIGNIFICANT LEY LINES IN ENGLAND

- A major ley line connects Stonehenge with Salisbury Cathedral and with a number of hillforts, tumuli, Stone Age settlements, and other ancient sites.
- One of the most celebrated and powerful lines, the St Michael's ley, runs diagonally from St Michael's Mount in the far southwest of England right across to the east of the country, passing directly through a great number of important sites, including Glastonbury, the important megalithic stone circle of Avebury, and the sites of more than sixty churches. It follows the line of the sunrise on the great Celtic festival of Beltane, celebrated on May Eve to mark the end of winter and the coming of spring and summer.

Similar wisdoms: Ley lines connecting shrines, temples, graves, sacred hills, and other sacred sites have been discovered all around the world. There are examples in South America, India, Egypt, and North America — for instance, the Nazca lines, Peru (right).

Dowsing

Dowsing is the search for underground water, minerals, or other objects, or even the answer to a yes or no question, using a divining device. Traditionally, a forked rod of hazel or apple wood was used, but a pair of L-shaped metal rods or a pendulum are also typical.

DOWSING TWIG

Water dowsers hold a Y-shaped hazel twig in both hands while crossing a field. When water is sensed, the twig points downward of its own accord. Dowsing can also reveal the presence of underground veins of metal.

Dowsing is an ancient activity. Cave paintings depicting a group of people watching someone who appears to be dowsing with a forked stick have been discovered in the Tassili-n-Ajjer mountains in the Sahara – they are estimated to be at least 8,000 years old. There is evidence that water dowsing was used by the ancient Egyptians, and the Chinese Emperor Yu is recorded as being a master dowser around 2200 B.C. The Old Testament of the Bible also contains references to dowsing; for example, Moses used a divining rod to find water in the desert when leading his people to the promised land.

Water dowsing is traditionally carried out using a forked hazel twig. When water is reached, the twig points downward without conscious effort by the dowser. One explanation for this is that the twig is pulled down by the water's magnetic energy field. When metal rods are used, they are held pointing forward and parallel; they swing inward or outward over the object of the search. A pendulum is a weight, made of wood, metal, glass, or crystal, suspended on the end of a cord. When it swings, the dowser interprets its direction. Each dowser may interpret the pendulum's movements differently. When asking a yes or no question, for example, some dowsers interpret clockwise rotation as yes and counterclockwise rotation as no; for others, swinging back and forth means yes, swinging from side to side means no.

PERMANENT RECORD

These ancient paintings from the Jabbaren Caves in the Sahara show male figures spinning small pouches attached to wooden sticks in an early depiction of dowsing.

Although the traditional hazel is still the stick of choice for many dowsers, various other materials, including laminated woods, nylon, metals, and carbon composites, are in use today, with excellent results in the right hands. Paul Sevigny, president of the American Society of Dowsers, uses Y- and L-shaped nylon rods to find oil and lost valuables.

locate points of high energy and record them on a map or plan. The points are then connected to show lines of electromagnetic force.

Dowsing also has more practical applications; for instance, it has been used to trace areas of negative energy or "geopathic stress" in buildings, which is believed by many to cause persistent illness in those who live or sleep there, often affecting one group of occupiers after another. Dowsing is also used to find lost objects and valuable underground commodities, such as mineral deposits, ores, precious metals, or even treasure. This type of dowsing is often performed over a map, and then confirmed *in situ.*

Some dowsers use a pendulum to determine issues of personal health, such as locating the source of disease or negative energy in the body, or even to determine the sex of an unborn baby. Dowsing is also widely used for seeking advice about personal problems or for help in decision-making. In such cases, the issues have to be phrased into questions that require a yes or no answer.

Similar wisdoms: Many cultures have their own traditional methods for finding places of positive energy in which to live. In Austria, for instance, there is an old custom in which farmers enclose a flock of sheep on the site of a proposed new home, and leave them overnight. They then observe where the flock sleeps, in the belief that the sheep will naturally move to the location with the most beneficial energies.

The Uses of Dowsing

Dowsing has long been thought of as a spiritual activity, and in the United States, dowsers are still referred to as "water witches." In the twentieth century, dowsing has gained considerable importance as a New Age activity, especially in Europe. It is used to detect and plot the earth's magnetic energies at sacred sites, and has been utilized extensively to reveal spiraling patterns of energy inside stone circles and to confirm the routes of ley lines. The dowser's method is to

Greek mysticism and mythology

The Greek myths and legends feature a pantheon of gods and heroes. The stories of their exploits, as described in Homer's *Iliad* and *Odyssey*, represent the journey through life. The ancient Greeks looked to the divine wisdom of the gods when making all important decisions, such as whether and when to get married, embark on a journey, or go into battle.

Dramatizations of the myths and legends of the gods played an important part in the ancient Greeks' spirituality. It was believed that the audience of a drama underwent a purging or purification of the emotions, known as catharsis, which helped them to develop an awareness of human progress and increased self-knowledge. A common mythological motif was that of the heroic journey, on which an individual had to carry out a series of tasks.

Consulting the Oracle

Methods of mystical divination, such as consulting the oracle, played a pivotal role in the everyday life of the ancient Greeks. The name oracle refers primarily to the priest or priestess through whom the gods were believed to speak, but also refers to the prophecies themselves and to the shrines where such divination took place. There were many oracular shrines in ancient Greece, the most famous being those of Zeus at

THE SCHOOL OF ATHENS

The ancient Greek Mystery Schools, such as the Athenean school depicted here by Raphael, employed a wide range of esoteric methods for the spiritual development of the individual. A common analogy for the journey through life was the path through a labyrinth.

Dodona and of Apollo at Delphi. Each shrine used a particular method of divination, ranging from the study of dreams, lightning, and animal entrails, to the flight patterns of birds.

The shrine dedicated to Zeus at Dodona was the oldest oracular site in ancient Greece. Visitors to the oracle scratched their questions onto strips of lead, hundreds of which have survived. Priests used a sacred oak tree for their prophecies, interpreting the rustling of its leaves and the noises made by brass vessels hung from its branches.

The Delphic oracle, dedicated to Apollo, was the most important in ancient Greece. A priestess spoke oracular messages while in a trance; these were then interpreted by a priest and given to the questioner in the form of verses and riddles. There is evidence that drugs such as opium, henbane, and hellebore were used to induce the priestess's trances.

The belief in oracular divination can still be found today in many cultures – for example, Haitian voodoo (or *vodou*) priests, African witch doctors, and Asiatic shamans.

The Mystery Schools

The great Greek philosophers and sages such as Pythagoras were deeply interested in the mystical lore of the East. They founded the Mystery Schools, specialist universities where life and death could be studied from a spiritual perspective. The subjects studied included the ancient wisdom and esoteric knowledge of India and Egypt; the great pagan library at Alexandria, which contained no less than 500,000 books on mystical subjects, provided a rich source of material.

The beliefs of the Greek mystics have become important concepts in New Age spirituality. They considered worldly goods and achievements unimportant, and life was seen as a journey of spiritual awakening, in which individuals could develop their highest potential and connect with the oneness of creation. The mystical lifestyle included initiation and purification ceremonies, acting, the study of numbers and geometry, and a vegetarian diet. These were believed to help the individual to uncover the divine, higher self that lay within. Rituals symbolizing death were widely used in initiation ceremonies, and were intended to help the initiate face mortality, abandon the ego, and connect with the immortal soul.

THE ORACLE AT DELPHI

Left: Delphi was the most important oracular site in ancient Greece. While in a state of shamanic consciousness, a priestess – also known as a sybil – consulted Apollo, the god to whom the shrine was dedicated, for guidance or understanding. A priest then interpreted her utterances in the form of a riddle or verse.

Celtic Wisdom

*Be not too wise, nor too foolish.
If you be too wise,
men will expect too much of you;
If you be too foolish,
you will be deceived.*

Instructions of King Cormac

The Celts

The Celts were an Indo-European people based in the Alpine regions of central Europe, who spread westward from around 1500 B.C. Their culture and beliefs gradually absorbed and replaced those of the shamanistic Neolithic people who came before them. Celtic art, mythology, and spirituality continue to exert a powerful influence on the Western world.

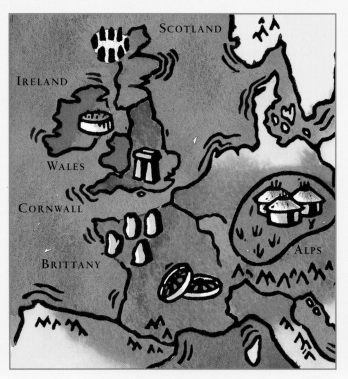

When it was at its peak, around 400 B.C., the Celtic realm extended right across Europe, from Asia Minor in the east to the Atlantic coast and the British Isles in the west. When the Romans advanced across Europe around the first century B.C., the Celts withdrew into strongholds in France and Britain. Today, remnants of the ancient Celtic culture can be found in Ireland, Scotland, Wales, Brittany, and Cornwall.

The main sources of inspiration in Celtic spirituality were the ancestors and memories of the past; the natural world and working in harmony with it; the connection between daily reality and the spirit realm, known as the Otherworld. Ancient Celtic folklore and divination methods are based on interpreting the signs and auguries found in nature in order to understand the present and explore the future, and this also forms the basis of much New Age spirituality.

KEY

 Celtic origins in central Europe, 1500 B.C.

 Greatest extent of Celts, 400 B.C.

 Surviving Celtic-speaking areas.

The Druids

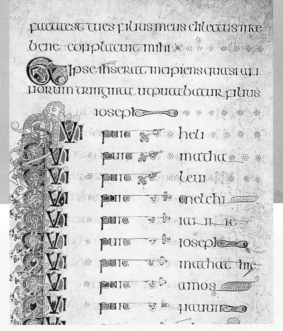

THE BOOK OF KELLS

The Book of Kells is perhaps the most celebrated of the great medieval illuminated Celtic documents. Weaving together text and elaborate visual images, it celebrated the wonder of creation, and expressed the profound spiritual connection between humankind and the natural world – a key theme of earlier Celtic spirituality.

The Druids were the religious leaders of the ancient Celts. They acted as shamans, magicians, healers, poets, priests, philosophers, judges, arbitrators, and counselors to kings.

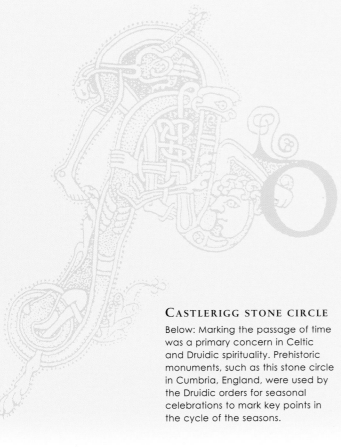

CASTLERIGG STONE CIRCLE

Below: Marking the passage of time was a primary concern in Celtic and Druidic spirituality. Prehistoric monuments, such as this stone circle in Cumbria, England, were used by the Druidic orders for seasonal celebrations to mark key points in the cycle of the seasons.

The Druids were instrumental in combining the wisdom of the Celts with the beliefs of the Neolithic cultures that had preceded them: both were based on the same pagan, pantheistic world view, consisting of a creator god, a mother goddess, and an array of nature gods. The Druids used the great megalithic structures, such as Stonehenge, for their spiritual practices and ceremonies. Contrary to popular belief, the Druids were not responsible for building these structures, but merely adopted them for their own uses.

Much of the Celtic culture survived the arrival of the Romans who, as elsewhere, were content to set up civil structures under which the existing order remained largely unchanged. The society that resulted from this cultural blending proved receptive to the spread of Christianity in the first and second centuries, but the new religion was subtly influenced by Druidic beliefs and practices, and Celtic Christianity developed as a distinct strand. A superb example of this mixing of Celtic and Christian spirituality is the highly ornamented *Book of Kells*, a medieval religious manuscript. Druidism was eventually suppressed by Christianity, but its practice continued underground for centuries. In the 1800s, Druidism underwent a revival among a small elite belonging to the romantic movement. Towards the end of the twentieth century, there was an explosion of interest in Druidism and Celtic culture as a whole.

Celtic divination

The Celts used a wide variety of divination methods, including casting Ogham sticks, interpreting dreams, illumination, and consulting the tree oracle. These divination methods provided the Celts with a way of understanding the natural energies affecting a situation, so that they could work in harmony with them.

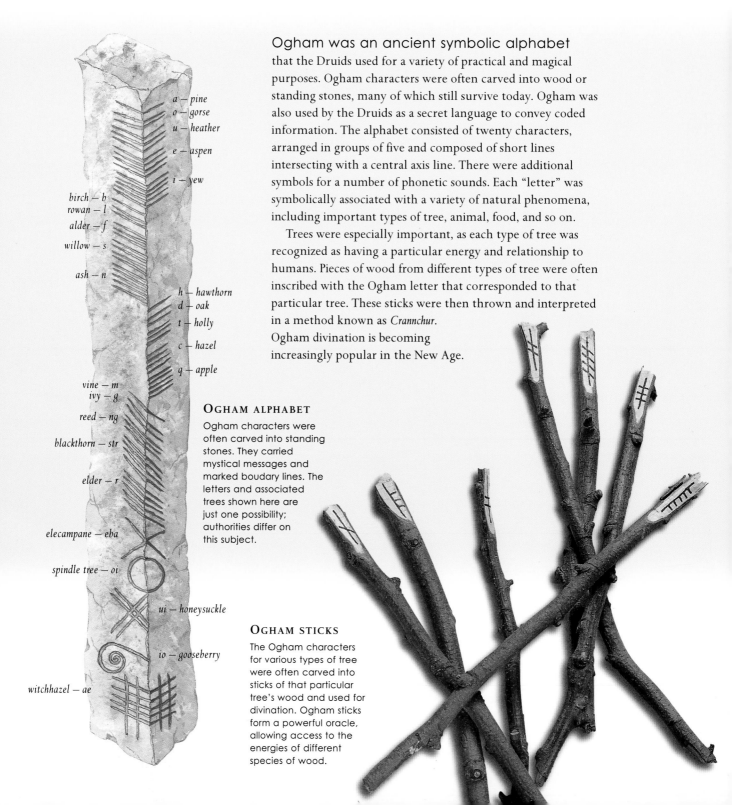

Ogham was an ancient symbolic alphabet that the Druids used for a variety of practical and magical purposes. Ogham characters were often carved into wood or standing stones, many of which still survive today. Ogham was also used by the Druids as a secret language to convey coded information. The alphabet consisted of twenty characters, arranged in groups of five and composed of short lines intersecting with a central axis line. There were additional symbols for a number of phonetic sounds. Each "letter" was symbolically associated with a variety of natural phenomena, including important types of tree, animal, food, and so on.

Trees were especially important, as each type of tree was recognized as having a particular energy and relationship to humans. Pieces of wood from different types of tree were often inscribed with the Ogham letter that corresponded to that particular tree. These sticks were then thrown and interpreted in a method known as *Crannchur*. Ogham divination is becoming increasingly popular in the New Age.

a — pine
o — gorse
u — heather
e — aspen
i — yew
birch — b
rowan — l
alder — f
willow — s
ash — n
h — hawthorn
d — oak
t — holly
c — hazel
q — apple
vine — m
ivy — g
reed — ng
blackthorn — str
elder — r
elecampane — eba
spindle tree — oi
ui — honeysuckle
io — gooseberry
witchhazel — ae

OGHAM ALPHABET

Ogham characters were often carved into standing stones. They carried mystical messages and marked boudary lines. The letters and associated trees shown here are just one possibility; authorities differ on this subject.

OGHAM STICKS

The Ogham characters for various types of tree were often carved into sticks of that particular tree's wood and used for divination. Ogham sticks form a powerful oracle, allowing access to the energies of different species of wood.

CELTIC CROSS
In the Celtic-Christian era, the
cross merged with earlier Celtic
motifs, fusing the power of these
two spiritual traditions. The
Celtic cross is a potent symbol
for believers in Celtic spirituality.

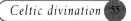

Dream Reading

"Incubatory Sleep" was another divination method widely
used by the ancient Celts. Temples were built with rooms
specifically dedicated to this purpose. A Druid initiate first
performed purifying rituals, then slept on his or her back with
a large stone on the abdomen. The resulting dreams were
expected to provide answers to particular questions or
problems, or to anticipate the future.

Illumination

Illumination was a way of embarking upon a shamanistic
journey. The Druid initiate entered a darkened place, such as
an underground chamber, and underwent sensory deprivation
for a period of hours or days. Many archaeologists now believe
that this may have been the function of ancient chambered
structures where there is no evidence of burial.

The Tree Oracle

Today, there are many New Age oracles, books, and card
sets based on traditional Celtic divination and self-awareness
techniques. The Celtic tree
oracle, for instance, is a modern
system of divination using a set
of cards, each card representing a
different tree. The cards are laid
out, much like tarot cards, and
interpreted in accordance with
each tree's unique characteristics.

TREE ORACLE CARDS

Trees were sacred to the
ancient Celts. Oak (*duir*)
was the most revered of all
Celtic trees; rowan (*luis*)
was the most magical tree;
and elder (*ruis*) was the tree
of life and death.

THE TUROE STONE

Many stones, such as this one in
County Galway, Ireland, were
engraved with elaborate
geometrical patterns that expressed
the connection between
humankind and the forces of nature
and patterns of time. They formed a
sort of symbolic map of the cosmos,
showing humanity's place within it.

THE HORNED GOD

This relief from an inner panel of the Gundestrup cauldron depicts Cernunnos, the Celtic god of wild beasts, with a pair of antlers and surrounded by an array of creatures. The cauldron, dating from around the first century B.C., was discovered in a bog in Denmark, where it had been placed as a ritual offering.

Animal wisdom

The ancient Celts believed that all animals, birds, and fish had a spiritual connection with humanity. Each creature was considered to have its own unique set of qualities, and all were regarded as sources of guidance, teaching, guardianship, and healing. Hunting was seen as a sacred activity, ruled by a strict code of respect that involved requesting permission from the relevant spirits before the kill.

THE BIRD OF ENCHANTMENT

The Celts considered the blackbird to be the bird of enchantment. In legend, its song had the power to put the listener into a trance, which allowed access to the spirit realm. The bird symbolizes self-awareness and self-discovery.

Animals were especially relevant to Celtic shamanism. Shamans wore the skins, horns, feathers, claws, bones, or teeth of particular creatures in order to access the animals' powers, which they used for hunting or to assist the shaman in looking after the tribe's health and spiritual well-being. Most practitioners focused on a specific magical animal or "familiar" – for example, the stag for help during the hunt; the bull for strength and courage; the hare for fertility and abundance; and the owl for insight and intuition.

A modern method of accessing the spiritual energies of animals involves the use of a set of cards, each bearing the image of a particular creature. These are laid out like tarot cards and interpreted according to each animal's qualities.

The Salmon of Wisdom

This tale is part of the Ossianic Cycle, a collection of epic stories that recount the heroic adventures of Finn mac Cumal in the third century B.C. Finn is the archetypal mythological warrior, seer, and poet, who set out on his journey as an innocent child and found wisdom along the way.

"At last, the youthful Finn came to learn poetry from the poet Finneces on the River Boyne. For seven years Finneces had been watching the salmon of Fec's Pool; for it had been prophesied of him that he would eat the salmon of Fec, whereupon nothing would remain unknown to him. The salmon was eventually found and caught, and Finn was ordered to cook it, but not to eat so much as a morsel of it. The youth brought the cooked salmon. "Have you eaten of the salmon, my lad?" said the poet. "No," Finn replied, "but I burned my thumb and put it in my mouth right away." It was thus that knowledge was given to Finn. From that time forward, whenever he put his thumb in his mouth, then whatever he did not know would be revealed to him."

A SOURCE OF WISDOM

The salmon was regarded by the Celts as the oldest animal of all, exemplifying the qualities of rejuvenation and youthfulness, and the search for wisdom and inspiration. In Celtic legend, it was the wisest of fish, for it fed on the hazelnuts of knowledge.

The Celtic year

The Celts believed that the cycles of the natural world and the celestial bodies held spiritual signficance and had a profound effect on humanity. The year was divided into two parts: the dark half and the light half. This division symbolized the recurring cycle of death, renewal, rebirth, and growth. The Celtic year began on October 31st, the start of the dark half of the year.

Each of the four seasons had its own distinctive characteristics and celebrations: Yule celebrated dormancy in winter; Eostre celebrated germination and growth in spring; Litha celebrated the heat of summer; and Halig celebrated harvest and fruitfulness in the fall. The four cross-quarter festivals marked the seasonal turning points, so each of these celebrations reflected the characteristics of the coming season. Imbolc was the time for purification and preparation; Beltane brought fecundity; Lughnasa celebrated the harvest; and Samhain was the time of preparation for darkness and winter. Beltane (marking the onset of the light half of the year) and Samhain (the onset of the dark half) were considered the most crucial points of the year, for on these occasions special access was possible between the everyday world and the spirit realm.

Most of the key dates in the Celtic year have been assimilated into the Christian calendar. For example, Eostre has become Easter and Yule has become Christmas. All Souls' Day and Halloween have replaced Samhain, and Candlemas has replaced Imbolc.

For people living in modern cities, it is difficult to maintain contact with the cycles of nature. However, many people in New Age circles are choosing to observe and celebrate these important occasions, using the Celtic year and rituals as a model. The celebration of the summer solstice on the eve of June 21st at Stonehenge is perhaps the most famous example of this.

THE SOLAR FESTIVALS

The solar year contained eight key dates: two solstices, two equinoxes, and the four cross-quarter days, which fell exactly in between the solstices and equinoxes.

October 31st:	**Samhain**	Halloween
December 21st:	**Yule**	Winter solstice
February 1st:	**Imbolc**	February eve
April 21st:	**Eostre**	Spring equinox
May 1st:	**Beltane**	May eve
June 21st:	**Litha**	Summer solstice
August 1st:	**Lughnasa**	August eve
September 21st:	**Halig**	Fall equinox

THE ASTROLOGICAL YEAR

Lunar cycles were also observed. In the system of Celtic tree astrology, each of the thirteen major trees related to a specific portion of the lunar year.

Birch	**Beth**	December 24th–January 20th
Rowan	**Luis**	January 21st–February 17th
Ash	**Nion**	February 18th–March 17th
Alder	**Fearn**	March 18th–April 14th
Willow	**Saille**	April 15th–May 12th
Hawthorn	**Uath**	May 13th–June 9th
Oak	**Duir**	June 10th–July 7th
Holly	**Tinne**	July 8th–August 4th
Hazel	**Coll**	August 5th–September 1st
Vine	**Muin**	September 2nd–September 29th
Ivy	**Gort**	September 30th–October 27th
Reed	**Ngetal**	October 28th–November 24th
Elder	**Ruis**	November 25th–December 23rd

THE CHANGING SEASONS

The recurring cycles of the natural year were crucially important to the Celts, not only for the timing of agricultural activities, but also for their spiritual potential. Each of the thirteen lunar phases was associated with a particular tree and its qualities, and formed the basis of an astrological system that is currently experiencing a revival of interest.

The Norse world

The peoples of the ancient Norse world include the Teutonic tribes of northern Germany and the Vikings of Scandinavia. The mythology, beliefs, and divination systems of the Norse people bear striking resemblances to those of the Celts, reflecting the two cultures' shared Indo-European roots.

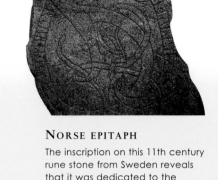

The ancient Norse and Celtic cultures shared a similar shamanic tradition, and both believed in the sacredness of the natural world and humans' special relationship with it. They used closely related divination methods, including dream reading, illumination, and the interpretation of auguries found in nature. With their characteristic straight lines, similarities can also be seen between the Norse runic script and the Celtic Ogham alphabet (though it is likely that they developed independently). Both alphabets were composed of straight lines, probably to make it easier to carve them into stone.

The runic alphabet is often known as the *futhark* alphabet, a term derived from the first six letters. The word rune itself comes from *runa*, the ancient Germanic term for a mystery or secret. Runes were used for a number of purposes, including written communication, divination, and as a focus for prayer.

Origins of the Runes

In Norse mythology, the runes were claimed to be a gift to mankind from Odin, the king of the Norse gods. The real origins of the runic script are unknown, but the first archeological runic inscriptions date from the third century A.D. There are three main forms of the script. The earliest is the northern Germanic futhark, consisting of twenty-four symbols, and this was in use between the fifth and eighth centuries A.D. The second is the Anglo-Saxon script, which was in use between the fifth and twelfth centuries A.D. Until about

ODIN, KING OF THE NORSE GODS
Odin was the creator god and principal deity in the Norse pantheon, and was derived from the Teutonic god known as Woden, Wodan, or Wotan. In legend, he discovered the runes while hanging from the World Tree. The legend reflects the magic qualities of the runic script.

900 A.D., it consisted of twenty-eight letters; afterward, it increased to thirty-three letters. The third main form of runic script was in use in Scandinavia and Iceland, also between the fifth and twelfth centuries A.D., and varied between fifteen and sixteen characters.

Over the centuries, other languages took precedence for communication, and runes were used more for divination purposes and as a secret language in which spells and folk remedies could be written. After the thirteenth century, the use of runes gradually declined in most areas, but continued in the far north — in Iceland, for example, where people were burned at the stake for using runes as late as the seventeenth century. The last of the great runemasters lived in Iceland around 300 years ago, after which the runic system was largely forgotten.

The twentieth century, however, has witnessed a huge resurgence of interest in the runes, and runestones are now one of the most popular tools of divination in the West.

Norse Legend and the Runes

Odin, in his search for wisdom, impaled himself upside-down on Yggdrasil, the World Tree, where he hung for nine days and nine nights. The magic runes came to him in what appears to be a shamanic trance, and he then gave them as a gift to all mankind.

For nine days and nights
I hung on a windswept tree,
Wounded by my own spear.
Of my self to my Self.
With neither food nor drink,
I saw into the depths of Being,
And from there took up the Runes,
Then fell, fainting.
Well-being and wisdom was my prize.

RUNIC STONE

Detail from a stone bearing runic inscriptions that was found in Rok, Sweden, dating from the first half of the ninth century A.D. It is the longest runic inscription discovered to date, and describes a young warrior who died in battle.

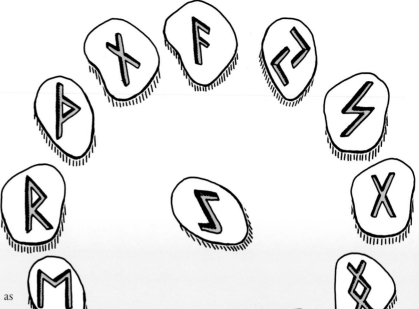

Consulting the Runes

The Norse people consulted the runestones for divination purposes on an everyday basis as well as on important occasions. The head of a family might use them to obtain advice about his work, or to discover the will of local deities. A high-ranking shaman might use them to induce states of altered consciousness, for healing, or to see and influence the future.

Most modern rune sets consist of twenty-five stones, one for each of the twenty-four letters of the runic alphabet and a single blank stone (a modern invention). Today, runes are not only used for predicting the future, but also for revealing the potential of the present – to help someone reconnect with their spirituality, regain a sense of destiny, or obtain guidance on a specific issue.

There are a number of ways of using the stones. First, an individual presents the problem issue or question. The runes are then laid out in one of a number of patterns or thrown on the ground. The symbols are then interpreted in relation to the problem. Through this process, the individual also symbolically accesses the particular power of each rune.

Circular Rune Reading

Lay all twenty-five runestones face down and move them around at random. Select thirteen stones and arrange them as if on a clock face, starting at 9 o'clock and working counterclockwise. Put the thirteenth rune in the center of the circle. Their positions – counting from 9 o'clock – refer to the subjects listed on the right. For this type of reading, the stones are "upright" when the tops are closest to the center of the circle.

POSITIONS

❶ = 9 o'clock, then count counterclockwise

⓭ = center

❶ Personality
❷ Material wealth
❸ Family
❹ Home
❺ Self-expression
❻ Health, environmen
❼ Love, marriage
❽ Inheritance
❾ Education
❿ Job, status
⓫ Pleasures, friendship
⓬ Psychic feelings
⓭ The questioner

Similar wisdoms: The *I Ching*, or Book of Changes, is an ancient Chinese system of advice and prediction. The book comprises 64 hexagrams – a stack of six horizontal lines, each representing either yin or yang – and accompanying sayings. For divination purposes, three coins are tossed six times to create the lines of a hexagram. The relevant saying is then interpreted.

Rune Interpretations

The simplest way to consult the runes is to place them all in a bag, then reach into the bag and remove three runes without looking at them. Turn over all three and refer to the meanings below to see what the runes have to say.

Ⓡ - The meaning when the runestone is reversed or inverted

FEOH
Wealth, property, financial gain, status, security
Ⓡ Loss

UR
Physical strength or skill, masculinity, determination
Ⓡ Physical or metaphorical weakness, missed opportunities

THORN
Protection, defense, caution, patience
Ⓡ Wrong decision, overcaution

AS
Authority, advice
Ⓡ Problems with authority figures

RAD
Change, movement, a journey, progress
Ⓡ Travel problems, unhelpful changes

KEN
Warmth, celebration, love, success
Ⓡ Lack of warmth or direction

GYFU
A gift, opportunity, partnership, teamwork
Ⓡ Loss, illegality, inability to perform a task

WYN
Joy, a water connection, luck
Ⓡ Depression, martyrdom

HAGAL
Sudden change, more often bad than good, disruption
Ⓡ Delay and disruption, even disaster

NYD
Basic needs, a warning to be patient, self-preservation
Ⓡ Emotional tension

IS
Standstill, plans or emotions frozen, a warning not to press on
Ⓡ The same but even more so, coldness, illness

GER
Ending and renewal, future growth
Ⓡ The same

EOH
Flexibility, avoiding problems
Ⓡ Indecision, regression

PEORTH
Mystery, the not-yet-known, psychic links
Ⓡ Fear, disappointment

EOLHS
Creativity, artistry, culture
Ⓡ A lack of these

SYGEL
Wholeness, life force, rest, recovery
Ⓡ The same, but perhaps overused

TIR
Victory through energy and heroism, passion
Ⓡ Weakness, a broken love affair

BEORC
Growth and fertility, beginnings, good news
Ⓡ Barrenness, illness, delay

EOW
Transportation, animals, changes, newcomers
Ⓡ Problems with any of these

MAN
A male authority figure, a warning to consult an expert before proceeding
Ⓡ Trouble with authority figures

LAGU
Feminine intuition, the fluidity of change, fertility
Ⓡ Paranoia, serious problems

ING
Fertility, family, good results
Ⓡ Lack of productivity, restriction

DAEG
Clarity, anything obvious, success, improvement
Ⓡ The same

ETHEL
Inheritance, the home, money matters
Ⓡ Problems with any of these

BLANK RUNE
Fate or destiny, things unknown – meaning affected by adjacent runes

Heroic journeys and spiritual quests

Myths and legends played a pivotal role in all ancient European societies, from Greek and Roman to Celtic and Norse. A common mythological motif was that of the heroic journey, on which an individual had to carry out a series of tasks in order to reach his or her goal.

The great epic hero tales, such as the Celtic legend of Taliesin, are mythological representations of the individual's rites of passage on the journey through life. Storytelling was the means by which early cultures expressed their identity and sense of history, and the ancient myths constitute the most powerful and sacred part of folklore. They represent the collective and individual quest for the ultimate meaning and purpose of life, while also incorporating historical records of real people and events. Ancient spiritual and cosmological wisdom are preserved in these stories.

New Age Significance

For millions of modern readers, the idea that myths are timeless models for understanding themselves has been suggested through the work of Joseph Campbell, a leading figure in the interpretation of ancient and traditional mythology. In his book *The Masks of God*, myths are described as poetic and dramatic images of our own spiritual potential, and as being especially applicable at times of initiation, transition, or crisis. Campbell shows that sacred stories everywhere contain archetypes of the collective unconscious, as well as meaning and inspiration on a more conscious day-to-day level.

Myth is the secret opening through which the inexhaustible energies of the cosmos pour into human cultural manifestation.
Joseph Campbell, The Hero with a Thousand Faces

THE RETURN OF ODIN

This stone, depicting Odin's victorious return, was found on the island of Gotland in Sweden and dates from the seventh century A.D. Sleipnir, Odin's eight-legged gray warhorse, can be seen in the top right of the procession.

The Legend of Taliesin

I wander through native lands
To help the clans.
Loudly I induce portent,
Seeking answer at the Strong Door.
I am old, I am young. I am Gwion;
I am universal.
I am gifted with perceptive spirit:
I remember the ancient wisdom.

This medieval illuminated manuscript shows Sir Galahad being shown to his place at the round table. The legend of the knights' search for the Holy Grail is one of the most enduring of all European folk tales.

The Legend of the Grail

The Grail is the lost chalice used by Jesus Christ at the Last Supper. It was supposed to have powers of transformation that could grant eternal life to its possessor. In the story, a vision of the Grail appears to the knights of King Arthur's round table, summoning them on a quest to find it. Many try, but none succeed. Parcifal, a lowly individual who has been brought up to reject the elitism of conventional knighthood, embarks on the quest and undergoes a series of tests and trials. Eventually he comes to the Castle of the Grail, where he has a vision of the Grail itself. However, he also meets the fearsomely wounded Grail King, whom he is unable to help. As a result, he has to wander desolately in the Wasteland for five years, suffering the same anguish that has physically wounded the Grail King. This represents the dark night of the soul or Underworld, the psychological condition in which an individual loses all sense of who he or she is. Eventually, Parcifal is reborn into his true nature and returns to his society, bearing the gift of his transforming vision of the Grail. Thus, the meaning of the quest lies in discovering one's true identity, with the ideal of compassion as the primary human value; the Grail itself symbolizes the goal of the spiritual journey.

The Meaning of the Grail Legend

Through this myth, the West was introduced to the idea that the true nature of reality lies within each individual's own heart and life. The archetypal quest is therefore an inward one, a crucial theme in New Age thinking today.

Interest in Arthur and the legends that surrounded him was renewed in the twelfth century. At this time, many epic tales about the king and his knights were written down and retold, complete with medieval pageantry and chivalry. Other writers on the European mainland then retold the legends of Parcifal. Later versions began to emphasize the quest for the Grail, notably Sir Thomas Malory's celebrated *Le Morte D'Arthur*. More recently, other authors and artists have continued to explore the legend. The great psychologist and mystic, C. G. Jung, regarded it as a key to understanding modern problems, both of the collective unconscious and the individual psyche. To him, it highlighted every person's need to move on from the inherited life – the collective ideals and beliefs of the group – to create the individual life that is his or her own.

Similar wisdoms:

Mythological questors in other parts of Europe include the Greek heroes Prometheus, Jason, Odysseus, and Theseus. Similar journeys and quests have also featured in accounts of actual historical figures, such as Jesus Christ and Buddha, whose stories have become mythologized.

Wise women and witches

Throughout Europe in the second millennium, the ancient traditions of female shamans gave way to a culture of "wise women" – country women who offered a service to their local community.

Wise women used ancient shamanistic techniques, which typically involved the interpretation of weather patterns, knowledge of herbs, and various types of healing and counseling. Some also claimed to communicate with animals – horse whispering, for example. As Christianity spread through Europe, these wise women were seen as a challenge to Christian beliefs and authority; they became known as witches and were persecuted.

WITCHES TODAY
The "ghost" of a witch at a tourist attraction in the US. While still often seen merely as figures of fun, witches and natural magic are now experiecing more serious interest.

A branch of contemporary paganism and witchcraft that is currently undergoing a revival is Wicca. The spirituality of Wicca is based on the natural world, and involves worship of the pre-Christian European deities. The earth itself is revered as the Great Mother. The purpose of Wicca is to put the individual in harmony with nature, and achieve practical goals such as healing by sacred, psychic, or magical means.

A key element in pagan ritual is the observation and celebration of the eight major annual festivals, as noted in the Celtic year (see pages 58–59). Ceremonies are often conducted outdoors, sometimes in a consecrated "magic circle," with fires, drumming, singing, and feasting. Observation of the moon's phases is also central to pagan practice.

CASTING HOROSCOPES
This illustration from a sixteenth-century pamphlet shows Ursula Shipton casting a horoscope for a client. "Mother Shipton" was an English seeress, whose predictions were published in 1642, after her death, under the title *Two Strange Prophecies*.

NEW MOON

WAXING MOON

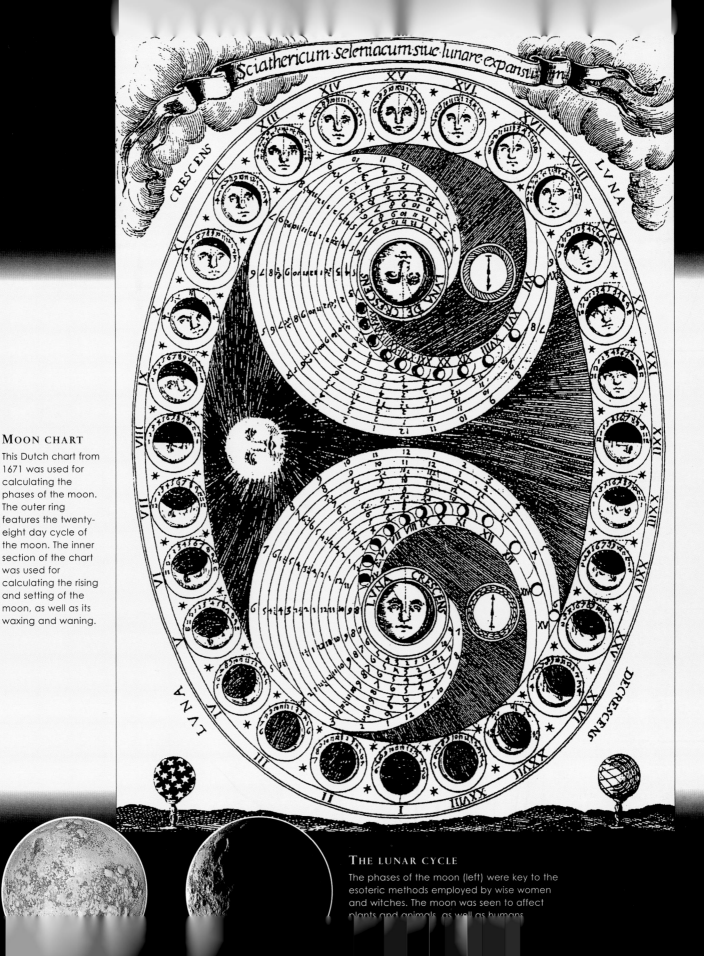

MOON CHART

This Dutch chart from 1671 was used for calculating the phases of the moon. The outer ring features the twenty-eight day cycle of the moon. The inner section of the chart was used for calculating the rising and setting of the moon, as well as its waxing and waning.

THE LUNAR CYCLE

The phases of the moon (left) were key to the esoteric methods employed by wise women and witches. The moon was seen to affect plants and animals, as well as humans.

Forest medicine

The use of plants for healing is probably the oldest form of medicine in the world. It was almost the only type of effective treatment until the eighteenth century. Medical herbalism is currently enjoying a revival in the West, as a result of public disenchantment with pharmaceutical drugs.

Angelica

Herbal medicine adopts a holistic approach to healing and shows ways of life enhancement, rather than just treating symptoms. Hippocrates, the Greek physician and "father of medicine," advocated the use of herbal drugs, along with fresh air, rest, and a healthy diet. He believed that this helped the body to strengthen its own "life force," so that it could eliminate its problems. Galen, a Roman physician, believed in using larger doses of Hippocrates' herbal remedies. The first European treatise on the properties and uses of medicinal herbs was *De Material Medica*, written in the first century A.D. by the Greek physician Dioscorides. This text was used well into the seventeenth century.

The use of plants for medicines was commonplace throughout Europe during the Middle Ages. Although the early Christian Church discouraged this, preferring faith healing, the Christian monks preserved many Greek medical texts. Monasteries, with their herb gardens, became local centers for herbal treatment. Herbal medicine was also practiced by midwives and wise women in their local communities. Fear and superstition were rife, however, and many magical properties were attached to herbal medicine, ultimately leading to the persecution and death of many wise women and herbal healers. A great loss of herbal remedies occurred during this time of persecution.

In the twentieth century, pharmaceutical drugs have become the predominant form of medicine in the West. However, 80 percent of the world's population still depends on herbal remedies. The importance of ancient herbal traditions is now being recognized in the West, as people seek to find a natural way of healing mind, body, and soul. As well as traditional herbal

THE ANCIENT HERBALIST

This illustration from Dioscorides' *De Materia Medica* shows the elderly apothecary and his apprentice collecting wild plants, then weighing and processing them in his laboratory.

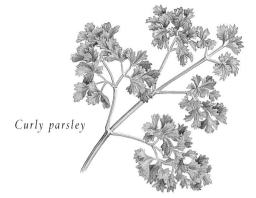

Curly parsley

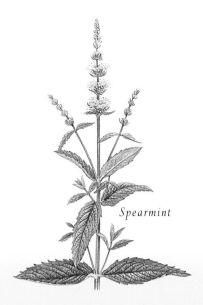

Spearmint

remedies, a number of related therapeutic methods are currently enjoying popularity. Aromatherapy is the therapeutic use of fragrant oils distilled from plants, which affect both the body and the emotions. They can be applied to the skin and from there are absorbed into the circulatory system, or their scents can be inhaled and carried by the olfactory nerves directly to the brain. Bach flower remedies were created by English physician Dr. Edward Bach in the 1930s, and consist of the essences of 38 plants, each of which has beneficial effects on the mind and moods. Homeopathy, developed in the late eighteenth and early nineteenth centuries, is based on the principle of "like cures like," and involves taking minute quantities of plant- or mineral-based remedies that in large doses produce effects similar to those of the disease being treated.

Herbal Lore

Herbs have been used as love charms, associated with gods and goddesses, and been part of birth, marriage, and death rites. Some were considered gifts from the gods, such as angelica in Scandinavia and mint in France and Spain.

Herbs that were hard to grow have the most lore associated with their planting. Parsley is a notoriously slow grower, and the legend is widespread that it visits the devil nine (or sometimes seven) times before sprouting. The recommended harvesting times were once governed by the moon's phases. Some herbs could only be cut with certain tools; for example, mint was never cut with iron.

Herbs have been used against evil spirits, nightmares, diseases, and witchcraft, and were often hung above doors and beds for protection. Rosemary was a popular protection in Spanish and Italian houses, and in Spain travelers wore it in their hats to ward off evil on the road.

Fortune-telling

One of the most significant influences on European divination methods came from the gypsies, who came to Europe from India from the ninth century A.D. onward. Gypsies were once thought to have originated in Egypt, and the word "gypsy" is in fact a corruption of the word Egyptian.

Gypsies traveled from India through the Middle East and into Europe, and were established everywhere by the sixteenth century. They call themselves Romanies, or "Lords of the Earth." Gypsies have always avoided intermarriage with outsiders, and have been persecuted throughout their history.

In their wanderings, the gypsies used many types of fortune-telling or "dikkering." They were traditionally skilled in older divination arts, such as herbalism, face reading, and the interpretation of omens from the stars and the behavior of animals and other natural phenomena.

FORTUNE–TELLING BY CARDS

This illustration, entitled *The Adventures of Tom, Jerry and Logick*, is by English artist Robert Cruikshank, c.1828. It shows an elderly woman of modest means reading the fortunes of well-to-do clients in her humble abode. Card reading was one of the methods of divination favored by the gypsies, and laid the foundations for the subsequent development of tarot card reading.

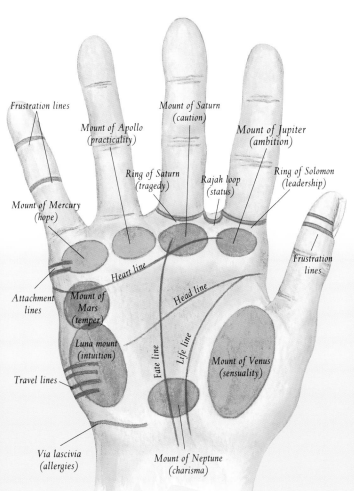

Frustration lines

Mount of Apollo
(practicality)

Mount of Saturn
(caution)

Mount of Jupiter
(ambition)

Ring of Saturn
(tragedy)

Rajah loop
(status)

Ring of Solomon
(leadership)

Mount of Mercury
(hope)

Frustration
lines

Heart line

Head line

Attachment
lines

Mount of
Mars
(temper)

Luna mount
(intuition)

Fate line

Life line

Mount of Venus
(sensuality)

Travel lines

Via lascivia
(allergies)

Mount of Neptune
(charisma)

CRYSTAL BALL

Telling the future by interpreting the shapes, patterns, and colors seen in a crystal ball is a form of "scrying," or divining. Crystal balls were traditionally made from clear quartz, but glass spheres are increasingly being used in the New Age.

Other Forms of Fortune-telling

Scrying is one of the oldest methods of divination, practiced by the ancient Egyptians and Babylonians, and independently developed in the Americas, Australasia, and Europe. It is the art of gazing at a reflective surface, such as a crystal ball or pool of water, and interpreting the images, symbols, figures, or events seen there. Tea-leaf reading is a recent practice in Europe, dating from the eighteenth century when tea became popular. Once the tea has been drunk, the reader examines the remaining leaves for patterns and interprets them. This art actually originated in China around 2,000 years ago. Playing cards are another popular divination tool used by fortune-tellers, especially on matters relating to love and romance.

Palmistry

Palmistry has been widely used as a form of divination since ancient times. It is referred to in manuscripts from India and China dated as early as 3200 B.C. In Europe, the Greek sage Aristotle promoted palmistry as a result of studying early Egyptian sources. In a reading, the lines on the palm are the primary focus, but the shape of the hand, fingers, and nails are also relevant. There are strong astrological associations with each line and part of the palm and fingers. The left hand represents inherited traits and potential, while the right indicates how this potential is currently being used.

Similar wisdoms: From ancient times, people have gazed into the surface of dark pools of water in order to gain insight. For instance, when a Dalai Lama dies in Tibet, visions are sought in a sacred lake to discover the birthplace of his reincarnated successor.

TEA-LEAF READING

Also known as tasseomancy, this involves interpreting the patterns of tea leaves. For example, a crescent moon shape means a love affair is coming; a tree means ambitions fulfilled; a bird means good luck is on its way.

The tarot

The tarot is widely regarded as the most highly evolved method of divination in European civilization. It first appeared in Italy during the Renaissance, but has been strongly influenced by a variety of much older sources, including the Jewish cabala, Celtic traditions, Indian tantric practices, teachings of underground Christian sects, and Egyptian secret wisdom.

GYPSY FORTUNE-TELLERS

Tarot was widely taken up by gypsy fortune-tellers who came to Europe from India in the fourteenth and fifteenth centuries to escape persecution. The gypsies were already acquainted with card reading, and used psychic or intuitive abilities in their readings. New Age tarot reading is a continuation of this ancient tradition.

The tarot grew out of a card game that was popular in Europe in the fourteenth century, and was probably carried back from the Middle East by Crusaders. Artists began to paint special allegorical images for the cards, with themes such as death or the wheel of fortune. Gypsies coming to the West at this time adopted the tarot for fortune-telling. In the late eighteenth century, occultists created tarot decks that incorporated elements from Egyptian and other magical sources, and this practice has continued ever since.

In the last quarter of the twentieth century, the popularity of tarot has exploded and the variety of decks has multiplied. There are now packs based on specific cultures, such as the Mayan, Australian Aboriginal, Tibetan, and Native American cultures; there are others based on subjects as diverse as

Arthurian legend, Jungian theory, the women's movement, and the works of Salvador Dali.

All tarot decks comprise two types of cards. There are the twenty-two trump cards, known as the major arcana, which illustrate life principles and the journey of the human soul from birth to enlightenment. There are also four suits of fourteen cards, each suit comprising cards from ace to ten, then knave, knight, queen, and king. The suits are commonly named swords, wands, cups, and pentacles, and are collectively known as the minor arcana.

Modern readings tend to focus less on prediction and more on psychological understanding. They attempt to explore the subconscious and to connect people's inner and outer experiences, in order to help them maximize their potential.

Reading the Tarot

There are many methods of setting out tarot cards when conducting a reading. The simplest is to draw three cards from the deck, representing the past, present, and future respectively. The major arcana foretell important events and strong emotions; the minor arcana reflect life's run-of-the-mill events and act as modifying factors on the major arcana.

Ⓡ = Meaning when card is reversed or inverted

The Major Arcana

0 THE FOOL
New experiences, new beginning requiring wisdom and courage
Ⓡ Recklessness, lack of motivation

1 THE COBBLER OR MAGICIAN
Creativity, imagination, willpower, confidence
Ⓡ Indecision, weak will, misuse of skills or powers

2 THE HIGH PRIESTESS
Wise judgment, strong creative abilities
Ⓡ Poor judgment, fear of commitment, conceit

3 THE EMPRESS
Domestic life, fruitfulness, positive achievement
Ⓡ Extravagance, laziness, wastefulness

4 THE EMPEROR
Worldly wealth and power, strength, confidence
Ⓡ Weakness, immaturity, obsession with fame and fortune

5 THE HIGH PRIEST
Kindness, desire to conform and gain social approval
Ⓡ Delayed ambitions, kindness to the point of foolishness

6 THE LOVERS
Loving relationship, friendship, harmony
Ⓡ Frustrated romance, infidelity, vacillation

7 THE CHARIOT
Struggle and triumph against the odds, prestige, unexpected news
Ⓡ Failure, collapse of plans, vanity

8 JUSTICE
Balanced objectivity and outlook, sincerity
Ⓡ Injustice, indecision, difficult adjustments

9 THE HERMIT
Enlightenment, the need to choose unfamiliar path
Ⓡ Mistaken advice, excessive caution

10 THE WHEEL OF FORTUNE
Unexpected events, wisdom from experience
Ⓡ Failed enterprise, difficult change

11 STRENGTH
Spiritual or physical strength, triumph
Ⓡ Weakness

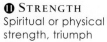
12 THE HANGED MAN
Willing sacrifice, lack of progress, stamina
Ⓡ Futile sacrifice, selfishness

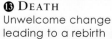
13 DEATH
Unwelcome change leading to a rebirth
Ⓡ Stagnation, fear of change

14 TEMPERANCE
Moderation, compromise, harmony
Ⓡ Conflict, lack of harmony

15 THE DEVIL
Self-indulgence, greed, controversy
Ⓡ Liberation, healing

16 THE TOWER
Unexpected events, temporary loss of stability
Ⓡ Destroyed ambition, boredom

17 THE STAR
Hope, love, rebirth, pleasure, satisfaction
Ⓡ Disapppointment, pessimism

18 THE MOON
Imagination, uncertainty, fluctuation
Ⓡ Minor deceptions avoided

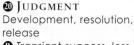
19 THE SUN
Satisfaction, gratitude, health, happiness
Ⓡ Lack of confidence, mild unhappiness

20 JUDGMENT
Development, resolution, release
Ⓡ Transient success, loss, delay

21 THE WORLD
Completion, reward, celebration, success
Ⓡ Disappointment, imperfect conclusion

The Minor Arcana

THE SUIT OF CUPS
Romance, friendship, creativity, sociability
Ⓡ Jealousy, pain, rejection, excessive love of luxury, self-preoccupation

THE SUIT OF WANDS
Creative integrity, security, positive relationships, inner development
Ⓡ Disrupted work, laziness, ignorance, romantic jealousy

THE SUIT OF PENTACLES
Generosity, financial reward, stability, success at work, craftsmanship
Ⓡ Meanness, covetousness, poverty, unemployment, isolation

THE SUIT OF SWORDS
Courage, strength, hope, peace amid strife, a successful journey
Ⓡ Spiritual suffering, loneliness, sacrifice, loss, defeat

ASIA

The vast expanse of the Asian continent has, from its earliest beginnings, produced a rich heritage of spiritual traditions. As the cradle of three of the world's major religions – Judaism, Christianity, and Islam – as well as home to some of the earliest documented shamanistic systems, it has made an immense contribution to New Age methods and practices.

Asia

For our purposes, Asia stretches from the eastern shores of the Mediterranean and the Ural mountains to the Bering Sea; and from the Arctic circle to the Himalayas. China, Japan, Tibet, and India have their own unique cultural heritage, and these are treated in separate chapters.

SPREAD OF ASTROLOGY AND EARLY SCIENCE FROM MESOPOTAMIA TO EUROPE

SPREAD OF EARLY CHRISTIANITY AND JEWISH DIASPORA TO EUROPE

SPREAD OF MONGOL CULTURE NORTH AND SOUTH

INFLUX OF BUDDHISM FROM TIBET

SPREAD OF ISLAM WEST TO AFRICA

SPREAD OF ISLAM EAST TO INDIA

The Mongolian Empire
During the rule of Genghis Khan (1167-1227 A.D.), the Mongolian Empire stretched from the Black Sea to the Pacific Ocean. His grandson, Kublai Khan, was a Buddhist, and under his rule Buddhism became widespread throughout the Empire.

The Black Stone
Muslims have a sacred duty to make a pilgrimage to Mecca. There, they form concentric circles around the Kaaba, which houses the Harju 'l-Aswad – the Black Stone – a meteorite thought to have been brought down to Earth by the Archangel Gabriel.

The Dead Sea Scrolls
Discovered in 1947 in various caves above the Dead Sea, these scroll fragments contain parts of every book of the Hebrew Bible (except the Book of Esther), as well assorted texts of the Jewish Qumran sect. Those scrolls found in the first Qumran cave are thought to have been written or copied between the first century B.C. and the first half of the first century A.D.

KEY

 Home of Islam in Arabia

 Center of astrology in Mesopotamia

 Herding shamanistic cultures

 Home of Judaism

 Maritime shamanistic settlements

 Centers of numerology

 Home of Christianity

 Original center of the Mongolian empire

OVOSIBIRSKIVE OSTROVO

East Siberian Sea

ARCTIC OCEAN

Chukchi Sea

ANCIENT MIGRATION FROM ASIA TOWARDS NORTH AMERICA

Indigirka

Kolyma

Bering Strait

Bering Sea

Sea of Okhotsk

PACIFIC OCEAN

N

Nomadic Shamanic Culture
Nomadic cultures dating back to Paleolithic times displayed examples of shamanic beliefs and customs, such as ritual burials. This type of spirituality is still found in parts of the Asian interior, including Siberia.

New Age Man
For some, Jesus Christ provides a model for New Age living, illustrating just how far the idea of interconnectedness can extend. As God incarnate, Christ embodies earthly man's links with the spiritual world, yet in his simple and nomadic existence he showed he was in touch with the lot of ordinary human beings.

The climate of Asia varies greatly from North to South, but extremes of temperature exist almost everywhere between winter and summer. The polar tundra of the far North gives way to a belt of coniferous forest that includes the Taiga; further South again lie the Steppes, a great expanse of grassland and scrub. The interior of the continent has very low rainfall, and much of it is desert. The southernmost countries – the Middle East and Asia Minor– are hot and very dry.

The indigenous peoples of this continent followed one of two basic traditional lifestyles, largely defined by climate and landscape. In the northern regions, survival was based on fishing, hunting, and herding animals such as caribou or reindeer. The South has traditionally been an area of agriculture and nomadic pastoralism. The predominant form of spirituality in these harsh climates was shamanism, and it is still in evidence in some parts of Asia today.

Many aspects of new age culture and practice owe their ultimate origins or influences to shamanism. Other shamanic practices have been directly adopted or revived as part of modern urban shamanism. Shamanic practices such as drumming, chanting, sweat lodge purification, and vision quests are becoming extremely popular today, as people search for ways of reconnecting to their remote spiritual roots, and step out of the clinical and logical modern mindset, and the disrespectful and destructive attitude to the natural world that is inherent in commercial and industrial growth. These methods have had a powerful influence on the spirituality of modern men's and women's movements.

Several of the world's great religions – Judaism, Christianity, and Islam, have their roots in Asia. Each of these has produced a more specialized mystical system: the Cabala, Gnosticism, and Sufism respectively, which have all regained importance in the New Age.

Asia has also produced two of the greatest systems for interpreting the connection between humankind and the cosmos, namely numerology and Western astrology.

Shamanism

Shamanism represents man's earliest attempts to control his environment and make an otherwise hostile world a safer place. It is based on the belief that the cosmos is guided by invisible forces, and it aims to influence these forces through formal ritual. The earliest indications of spiritual awareness are found in Neanderthal caves in central Asia.

The word shaman is a native Siberian word meaning "he who knows." Within the New Age movement, the term is now generally applied to spiritual leaders from ancient cultures across the world, from the Aborigines of Australia to the bush people of the Kalahari Desert in Africa. As ancient cultures experienced an intimate relationship with their landscape, so shamanistic practice reflects these similarities. Shamanism was the first belief system to embrace the concept of a human soul, and to hold that well-being is connected to the spirit world.

The Role of the Shaman

Shamanism is based on an animistic outlook that regards the natural world as alive with different energies, interpreted as spirits or divinities. These spirits inhabit trees, streams, mountains, animals, and the earth.

　　The shaman transcends personal identity, and acts on behalf of the whole tribe or society as an intermediary between life and the metaphysical spirit. This is achieved through shamanic ecstasy, a trance induced by drumming, dance, singing or chanting, fasting, or herbal stimulants. In this state, the shaman's soul enters the spirit world, communes with ancestors, gains information about sickness or disaster, or enlists allies to help with healing, magic, or divination. The transcended realm is sometimes presented as a lower world into which the shaman descends, and sometimes as an upper world into which he flies.

SACRED TOOLS

Left: Rattles and drums are commonly used in shamanistic rituals. Usually made from animal materials – fur, skin, and feathers – they also include metal attachments, such as bells and chimes, to create sympathetic tones for ritual chants, verse, and song.

DREAM STATES

Right: One of the shaman's roles is to read dreams. This sixteenth-century Iranian image is a shamanic reading of a dream, showing a man, surrounded by fishes, achieving spiritual fulfillment by awakening his five senses of perception.

ANIMAL MASKS

Left: Shamans wear masks and costumes to help them communicate with their animal spirits, as shown by this tribal motif. Traditionally, the animals with spiritual significance were those that lived and were hunted in the same region as the community, such as the buffalo, reindeer, or caribou.

The shaman sees all things as interconnected in a web of beingness, in which everything affects everything else.
Leo Rutherford
New Age Shamanistic Writer

The tribal shaman is born into his vocation, rather than choosing it through free will. Shamans are a dynastic group – they are usually sons or daughters of existing shamans, or specially selected apprentices whose gifts are brought out by the spirits. With power and prestige in the community, the shaman works alongside the elders to provide advice on all aspects of life.

Similar wisdoms: The American medicine man has an equivalent role to the Asian shaman. This 1876 illustration by George Catlin shows the medicine man in ceremonial wolf skin, holding a tambourine and spear. Catlin was one of the first Europeans to visually record tribal lore and provide a detailed account of spiritual rituals.

KHANTY SHAMAN

Left: This shaman, shown standing, is from the Khanty people of Siberia. He wears his ceremonial fur head-dress and animal-tooth necklace, and holds a ritual drum and rattle. The two Khanty women, seated, also wear traditional dress, which shows the European folk influences on western Siberia.

The goddess

The goddess figure dominates the ancient religions of the Middle East and West Asia. Holding the title Great Mother of the Gods or Mother Goddess, she is the ultimate symbol of the earth's fertility. She was worshipped under many names and attributes, but essentially she was the creative force in nature, responsible for the renewal of life.

Asian cultures wove elaborate stories for their goddess figures, illustrating their role in the world's creation. The name of the goddess varied across the region – in the ancient lands of Phrygia and Lydia she was known as Cybele, among the Babylonians and Assyrians, she was Ishtar, and in Syria and Palestine, she appeared as Astarte. Cultural exchanges with ancient Greece and Rome took the goddess figure across into Europe where, centuries later, she reappeared in the Virgin Mary cult that developed within early Christianity.

Ishtar and Tiamet

From ancient Babylonia, the goddess Ishtar is the goddess of morning and evening, causing arguments between brothers and friends. She is known as the Star of Lamentation, the sovereign of the entire world through love's omnipotence. As the goddess of love, she was said to treat her lovers and fellow gods cruelly, and fostered a cult of sacred prostitution. One of the most famous legends of Ishtar is her descent into the underworld in search of her lover Tammuz and her triumphant return to earth.

The goddess Tiamet, from the same regional tradition, also portrays both gentle and aggressive traits. Her mythology states that creation stems from water, when the sweetwater god Apsu fused with the saltwater goddess Tiamet. Tiamet gave birth to creation and won the subsequent war with Apsu using armies of serpents, scorpion-men, and dragons.

The New Age Goddess

Although male-oriented deities began to eclipse goddess worship after 4000 B.C., God remained female for many cultures of West Asia and the Middle East. Goddess spirituality is still a powerful influence on modern feminists, psychotherapists, pagans, and eco-activists. The same philosophy has fostered non-hierarchical management structures in the workplace, and the establishment of female icons represented through the mass media.

GODDESSES PAST AND PRESENT

Right: The cult of the goddess Ishtar originated in Sumeria, southern Mesopotamia, where she was known as Inanna. This statuette shows her with characteristic wide eyes and head-dress.
Left: Pacifist protester at the U.S. airbase, Greenham Common, England. Women were at the vanguard of the Cold War pacifist movement, and focused their attention on nuclear bases, where they established semi-permanent protest camps in the early 1980s. As a women-only movement, they helped fashion a New Age feminist discourse.

Christianity

Christianity is the major religion of the Western world, and its influence cannot be overestimated. Secular New Agers, who may not even regard themselves as religious, now view its early teachings as a source of transformative practices.

HEALING POWERS
Above: The image of Christ the healer rings true for New Agers, who have embraced spiritual healing arts, such as Reiki.

Christianity began as an offshoot of Judaism and, for his followers, Jesus was believed to have fulfilled the biblical prophesies of the Messiah King. At first, Christianity was just another sect within Judaism, but it quickly drew new members and spread to the surrounding regions outside Palestine. From the outset, Church leaders had to contend with established pagan beliefs and practices, and these caused sectarian divisions within the early movement. These heresies, commonly known as Gnosticism, included both pre-Christian beliefs and radical interpretations of the new doctrine. In an attempt to rediscover the essence and truth behind their faith, New Age Christians are turning once again to these philosophies.

EARLY CHRISTIAN TRADITIONS

Left: First built in 635, the monastery at Lindisfarne, northern England, was the first establishment of Celtic Christianity, fusing Christian beliefs with the established customs of the native Celts. Pope Gregory the Great (540–604) was instrumental in bridging the gap with non-Christian traditions, urging missionaries to take over pagan temples and festivals, and give them a Christian meaning.

Above: Church of Mystra St. Theodore, Greece. The early Greek Church was under the control of the Roman, then Byzantine empires. Early churches retained the hallmarks of classical Byzantine architecture, and there were theological crossovers from the worship of the pagan sun god to Jesus Christ.

Fusing Ancient Beliefs

As Christianity spread through the Roman Empire, its mission was to convert the native peoples under its power, including the range of nationalities serving in its armies. However, church leaders at the Council of Constantinople of 381 acknowledged that "the churches of God among the barbarian races must be governed according to custom," signifying that the language and culture of pagan nations were to be acknowledged. The Roman Empire itself was reluctant to give up its emperor cult and local deities for the god of the Jews, who shunned idols. As pagan nations converted to Christianity, they diluted the official doctrine with their own cultural traditions.

Heretical groups within Christianity contained elements of Platoism, Zoroastrianism, and Judaism, promoting ritual magic and the use of amulets to crush evil powers. Some Gnostics promoted an ascetic lifestyle to protect the soul, while others favored a less moral ethic. Most accepted the concept of redemption, although not all accepted Christ as the redeemer. Gnostics, such as Marcion, stressed the moral contradictions between the Jewish bible and the Gospels.

New Age Christianity

Gnostic sects serve as an example of how theological discussions about the very basis of Christianity were still possible before the doctrine was finalized. The range of views within Gnosticism are now a source of inspiration to New Age Christians seeking the pure essence of Christianity. Sites of early Christian missions have become pilgrimages, while Christian settlements have been established to rekindle the idealism of early Christianity, such as at Findhorn, in Scotland. Even within mainstream Christianity, Church leaders are always looking for new ways to make their message relevant to the New Age generation, and looking back to the original heretics provides an opening for discussion about personal and communal spiritualism.

ANGEL CULT

Left: Angel cults evolved in Christianity as both protective guardians and evil figures. This mosaic from the apse of San Vitale, Ravenna, Italy, glorifies bishop Ecclesius by showing him side by side with Christ, angels, and saints, proudly holding his new church. Angels figured largely in Gnostic theologies, particularly those of Collosian Christians, who identified with the heavenly bodies.

Jewish mysticism

The Jewish mystical tradition is based on esoteric rabbinic commentaries designed to enhance personal spirituality and take man closer to God. Like its mystical counterparts in the Christian and Islamic faiths, its emphasis is on the individual experience, employing sophisticated visualization techniques and secret codes.

After the destruction of the second temple, the Jewish people became a diaspora, and moved through the Babylonian empire, Europe, and Asia, taking their faith with them. They adopted elements of their host nations and gave back their own philosophies and world view in return.

The primary aim of Jewish mystics was to venerate God through the study and interpretation of biblical texts. As communities moved from one region to another, they imbued the ideas of ancient Rome, Greece, and Babylon. Just as these

THE WESTERN WALL, JERUSALEM

Below: As the last remaining outer wall of the second temple (destroyed 70 A.D.), the Western Wall is a place of pilgrimage for Jews across the world, and traditional prayer services still make reference to the original rituals and offerings held in the temple, Details of the temple's holy of holies, containing the Ark of the Covenant, have always been shrouded in mystery, known only to the high priests. The priestly classes retain a key role in traditional Judaism, despite the loss of the temple, and perform blessings for the community during festivals.

HANDS OF GOD

Left: Hand amulets were traditionally used among Middle Eastern and North African Jews to protect against the Evil Eye. Fashioned from silver, brass, or ceramic, they were hung outside homes as talismans. The hand was commonly known as a Hamsa, meaning five in Arabic, and was treated in the same way as the Hand of Fatima symbol used in Islamic culture. Right: Traditionally, Jerusalem stone masons carved a hand into the houses that they built.

COLOR OF HEAVEN

Above: The picturesque city of Sfat, Israel became a center for Jewish mystics after the expulsion of the Jews from Spain in 1492. Doors are traditionally painted blue, the color of heaven, to ward off the Evil Eye.

ancient cultures discussed the relative power of their deities, so early Jewish mystics analyzed the relative power of human endeavor and God's word, following on from the Bible, which itself contains mystical elements within its narrative.

Mystical experiences were traditionally confined to small esoteric groups who transmitted their ideas by word of mouth. The Sepher Yetzira, or Book of Creation, is said to be the oldest record of Jewish mysticism, and was apparently composed sometime between 300–600 A.D., coinciding with the codification of Jewish Scripture, Liturgy, and Oral Law. Significantly, it was written in the same era as other major mystic teachings: the Vedic scriptures, the Hammurabi Babylonian Laws, the Egyptian Book of the Dead, and Pythagorean theories on the cosmos. Some of the early mystical writings survive in mainstream Jewish liturgy, while others are being reintroduced by New Agers, both from the orthodox and liberal Jewish denominations.

SIGNS AND WONDERS

Left: *Belshazzar's Feast* by Rembrandt. The holiness of the Hebrew language is confirmed by biblical images of the sacred letters. According to the Bible (Daniel 5), King Belshazzar of Babylon held a feast where this message appeared on the wall. Daniel interpreted it as a prophecy of doom and that night the kingdom fell to Cyrus. As the Bible was said to be given in Hebrew, it has developed a mystique of its own, expressed through the process of gemmatria, or Hebrew numerology.

Jewish mysticism 85

The Cabala

Cabala is the Jewish mystical tradition. The term comes from the Hebrew word for "received," as the sages' teachings were received by successive generations. Cabala is an attempt to understand God and its implications for humanity.

Since its early development in the third century A.D., the Cabala has evolved and responded to the challenges of each era. It became a source of secret wisdom and power that was tempered with caution and understanding. It is still used to understand human consciousness and the spiritual evolution of the individual through meditation and study. The long-standing cultural exchange between rabbinic authorities and Christian and Islamic clergy in Asia and Europe has meant that Cabala has had an enormous influence on other spiritual traditions, Western astrology, Tarot, and alchemic philosophy.

SAYINGS OF THE MYSTIC FATHERS

Above: Studying the holy scriptures was, and still is, the primary occupation of Jewish mystics. Abraham Abulafia (b 1240 A.D.) developed the technique of rearranging the letters of words to reveal mystical meanings. The simple structure of the Hebrew language made it particularly suited to this exercise.

The Tree of Life

The Tree of Life is a key symbol within Cabala, and is a living model for personal development. It consists of ten sefirot, or archetypal numbers, related in a grid of interaction. These represent the different characteristics of God and their effects throughout creation. The pattern of these interactions can be read in different directions. The ultimate divine essence is at the top, followed by the middle and lower realms of reality, including the material world where humanity exists.

For instance, the first sefira (singular), Keter, is at the top of the Tree of Life. Meditating upon it can give access to the divine characteristics that it embodies. These characteristics include Divine Will, the source of spiritual inspiration, and the nothingness from which everything ultimately originates.

Similar wisdoms:

Trees are a powerful spiritual symbol in ancient mythology. Siberian Shamanism refers to the "cosmic tree" which must be ascended in all shamanistic journeying, and this image occurs in Norse legends and mythology. The Biblical Tree of Knowledge (shown) has more negative connotations, as it prompted the fall of Adam.

Cabala Today

New Age Cabalists have developed meditation and chanting techniques to experience the Cabala, using both English and Hebrew transliteration. These techniques differ from traditional Jewish Cabalists, whose study and meditations are primarily devoted to the worship of God and the Bible.

READING THE TREE

The sefirot align in three vertical columns, with 22 visible pathways linking them. There are other invisible links, which can only be experienced through meditation. The layout is based on the three divine principles: Primordial Will, Mercy, and Rigor. Primordial Will is said to hold the balance of Emanation, while Mercy expands the worldly energies, and Rigor constrains their flow. The sefirot can be read as vertical pillars, triangles, horizontal planes, or using a zigzag route.

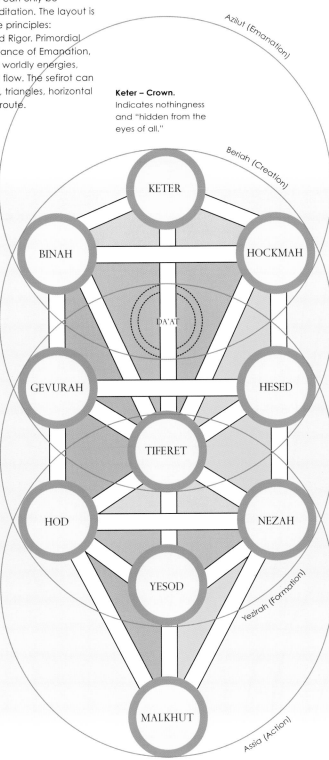

Azilut (Emanation)

Beriah (Creation)

Keter – Crown.
Indicates nothingness and "hidden from the eyes of all."

KETER

Binah – Understanding.
Indicates intellect or reason. Within this area also lies Da'at, the invisible sefirah, representing knowledge from God.

BINAH

HOCKMAH

Hockmah – Wisdom.
Indicates fear and thought.

DA'AT

Gevurah – Judgement or Power.
Indicates outer emotion, discipline, and discrimination.

GEVURAH

HESED

Hesed – Mercy
Indicates loving kindness, tolerance, inner and active emotion.

Tiferet – Beauty.
Indicates equilibrium and balance.

TIFERET

HOD

NEZAH

Nezah – Endurance.
Indicates eternity, determination, instinctive and impulsive elements.

Hod – Glory
Indicates the passive, cognitive, and controlling elements.

YESOD

Yezirah (Formation)

Yesod – Foundation
Indicates the generative and reflective. This sefira contains all the energies of the other sefirot and is said to be the mirror of reality.

MALKHUT

Assia (Action)

Malkhut – Kingdom or Presence
At the bottom of the Tree of Life, this sefira complements Keter at the top, and represents Shechinah, which is the presence of God in the material world.

THE FOUR WORLDS

The Cabala divides the universe into four worlds, inspired by Isaiah 43:7, "Every one that is called by My Name, for My Glory I have Created him, I have formed him: indeed, I have made him." The words *called*, *created*, *formed*, and *made* form the basis of a complete Cabalistic world view. The worlds are Azilut (Emanation) at the top, followed by Beriah (Creation), Yezirah (Formation), and Assia (Action) at the bottom, which is the material world.

MAGIC SQUARE
The magic square is a key symbol in medieval numerology, where the sum of digits along each row add up to 15.

Numerology

The language of numbers has deep significance in the ancient cultures of the Middle East. It is used for reading new meaning into holy texts, and as a divination tool in conjunction with astrological systems.

Numerology is a worldwide system and lies behind many other systems of divination. The mystical possibilities of numbers and geometric forms have fascinated societies throughout the ages, and are undergoing a New Age revival. The practice is concerned with gaining deeper knowledge of spirituality and the patterns of life. Numbers are believed to be the only constants in the world, remaining the same throughout time, space, and emotion. The study of numbers unlocks the laws of divine mathematics, as nature represents the geometric expression of higher, spiritual intelligence.

Origins and Development

Numerology was widespread in the ancient cultures of the Middle East and ancient Greece, where basic methods were used to interpret dreams and complement astronomical and astrological readings. There was a cultural exchange of numerological systems, to the extent that the second temple in Jerusalem used Greek as well as Hebrew symbols in its inscriptions. From the second century A.D., more advanced systems developed in the Babylonian empire by court scientists and within Cabalistic academies, who used it as a means for finding mystical meaning in the scriptures. As each one of the 22 Hebrew letters has a numerical value, the Cabalists sought meaning in the numerical value of Biblical words. Later Christian scholars also used numerology to find new meanings in the Bible. Seven is regarded as a particularly holy number as there are so many references to it in the scriptures.

Pythagorean numerology was a simpler system, and is now the most widely used system, focusing on the numbers one to nine. The numbers zero and ten are not used in Western numerology – zero is a relatively late addition to Western science, and ten is regarded as a composite number.

Links with Other Disciplines

Color therapists link numbers to individual colors, as both have set vibrational frequencies. In addition to the seven colors of the rainbow, silver and gold are also associated with the numbers one to nine. For every astrological system, there is a numerological system associated with it. The systems are not interchangeable, as each one has its own rationale and process of analysis. For example, in the Hindu system, the numbers one to seven are said to harmonize

ABRAHAM AND THE THREE ANGELS
Biblical scholars regard three as the divine number. There are many examples which form this theory: Abraham was visited by three angels, as depicted by this Italian manuscript of 1480, the Jewish temple at Jerusalem was built in three days, there are three gifts of the spirits, the resurrection of Christ took place after three days. The Holy Trinity is the most famous spiritual application of the number three.

The King built the wall of Horseabad
16,283 cubits long to correspond
with the numerical value of his name
Inscription of Sagon II (727–707 B.C.)
Ancient Babylonian ruler

Number is the ruler of form and ideas
and is the cause of gods and demons
Pythagoras' Sacred Discourse
c. sixth century B.C.

with the attributes of the seven planets and the days of the week, while the numbers eight and nine are given additional qualities.

The knowledge of planetary cycles is invaluable to numerologists who use the discipline for divination. An understanding of psychology, palmistry, and graphology are also essential, especially for individuals who want to change their names or address.

Similar wisdoms: Middle Eastern numerology has counterparts in the Chinese I Ching and the Vedic square from India (below). The table on the left is used as a base for calculating the table on the right. The numbers on the outside rows of the left-hand square are multiplied, then the numbers which comprise the total are added together to form the right-hand table. For example 4 x 4 = 16, then 1 + 6 = 7. For divination, each number is assigned a specific meaning and linked to the letters in an individual's name and birth date.

SACRED GEOMETRY
Above and left: The geometric application of numbers is most apparent in natural forms, such as this ammonite fossil, and ancient cultures viewed this as a manifestation of the divine. Man-made representations of natural forms, like the architecture of the Guggenheim Museum, New York, aim to evoke the same divine power and impact.

1	2	3	4	5	6	7	8	9
2	4	6	8	10	12	14	16	18
3	6	9	12	15	18	21	24	27
4	8	12	16	20	24	28	32	36
5	10	15	20	25	30	35	40	45
6	12	18	24	30	36	42	48	54
7	14	21	28	35	42	49	56	63
8	16	24	32	40	48	56	64	72
9	18	27	36	45	54	63	72	81

1	2	3	4	5	6	7	8	9
2	4	6	8	1	3	5	7	9
3	6	9	3	6	9	3	6	9
4	8	3	7	2	6	1	5	9
5	1	6	2	7	3	8	4	9
6	3	9	6	3	9	6	3	9
7	5	3	1	8	6	4	2	9
8	7	6	5	4	3	2	1	9
9	9	9	9	9	9	9	9	9

Applications of Numerology

Western numerology readings have various applications for the individual.

The name number is worked out by assigning numbers to each letter of the name, then adding these together. The letter A is represented by number 1, B is 2, C is 3 and so on, coming to the letter I which is 9. Then the sequence repeats, with J being 1 again, K as 2, and so on. The resultant number is reduced to a single figure by addition, and interpreted according to standard charts of meaning.

The birth number derives from the date of birth, by adding together the digits of the day of the month, the number of the month, and the full number of the year. This number is reduced to a single figure, then interpreted. The birth number relates to an individual's overall life pattern. It reveals the most stable personal attributes – the ones least affected by outside influences and most strongly related to the unconscious mind. The strongest impact of this influence occurs after the age of thirty – the time of the "Saturn Return." This is the time of new beginnings, as it represents the time when Saturn, in its thirty-year cycle, is in the same position as at the time of birth.

Psychological makeup is indicated by the psychic number, which is derived from only the day and month of birth. It reveals the more unstable personality traits, such as patterns of thought, desires, and ambitions. These are the qualities that are influenced most strongly by the conscious mind, and are most affected by external influences.

Numerology helps individuals gain a better understanding of their relationships – for instance, their lovers, family members, bosses, or employees. It also helps explain the dynamics of a relationship through the interaction of the two number sets.

Lastly, the interaction of past, present, and future can be understood by studying the cycles of fate, or life patterns. For example, it is possible to detect an eighteen-year cycle in which major life events repeat themselves, and also an intermediate nine-year cycle of opposite patterns. It is also possible to use an individual's particular numbers to work out which years of his or her life have special numerological significance.

NAME NUMBER

In the widely-used Pythagorean system, each number corresponds to a letter of the alphabet:

1	2	3	4	5	6	7	8	9
A	B	C	D	E	F	G	H	I
J	K	L	M	N	O	P	Q	R
S	T	U	V	W	X	Y	Z	

So, the name number for John Smith is calculated like this:

$$1 + 6 + 8 + 5 = 20$$
$$1 + 4 + 9 + 2 + 8 = 24$$

$$2 + 0 = 2$$
$$2 + 4 = 6$$

Total of both names: $2 + 6 = 8$

John Smith's name number: 8

If your total of both names is a two figure number it goes through a further process:

so 15 would become: $1 + 5 = 6$

WHAT'S IN A NAME?

Letters in a name are converted into numbers, then added together to provide a single number between one and nine. Some systems state that each number has its own vibrational frequency in nature, and these have their own personality attributes.

BIRTH NUMBER

To calculate the birth number, add together the day, month, and year of birth to make a single whole number.

So, if John Smith's birth date is 14 September 1971, calculate his birth number like this:

$$1 + 4 + 9 + 1 + 9 + 7 + 1 = 32$$
$$3 + 2 = 5$$

John Smith's birth number: 5

BIRTH ATTRIBUTES

Birth numbers complement name numbers, and indicate primal characteristics evident at birth.

Traditional Numerological Interpretations

As the first number, this represents the origin, the solitary eminence of the Sun, the creator. It is a powerful number, associated with strong masculinity and leadership. People with this number have a tendency to be inventive, determined, and possessive of a pioneering spirit. Along with power goes responsibility, and unless the person is careful, there is a risk of falling into selfishness and egotism. If their schemes fail, they may become aggressive or introverted; even if their schemes succeed, they may become overbearing,

Just as One is associated with maleness, so is Two with femininity, being gentle, intuitive, harmonious, and romantic. It is symbolized by the Moon and suggests a gentle creativity and an ability to mix well with other people, but an inability to be forceful, to make decisions, or to carry tasks through to their necessary conclusions; more mental power than physical.

Threes are creative and disciplined people, associated with the planet Jupiter. Growth, success, luck, happiness, and fertility are suggested, though on the negative side the person may also be gossipy, moody, over-critical, sometimes rather shy, pessimistic, or unimaginative, and prone to leaving jobs half done. You will get on especially well with other Threes.

There is a completeness in Four, because mathematically it is a square. It is associated with the Earth and its four seasons, and people under its influence tend to be very down-to-earth and systematic. Yet there is also an earthbound side to these people, who may be over-fussy about small details, lazy, weak, and prone to worrying too much. Occasionally, a Four will have a stubborn, rebellious streak.

Under the influence of the planet Mercury, Five represents the senses. There is activity, change, a hatred of routine, a need for novelty, and a reputation for unpredictability. Such people are energetic, adaptable, intelligent, and quick to learn. They may be too demanding of others, too impulsive, prone to spreading themselves too thin through too many projects at once. They make friends very easily, but are difficult to live with.

Six is the number of emotions, ruled by Venus, planet of love. Mathematically, it is a "perfect number," because it is the sum of its factors, 1, 2, and 3. People under its sway tend to be reliable and well-rounded. There is a love of home, of peace and beauty, and harmony. Sixes tend to be artistic, and good with children and animals. They may also be too sympathetic, self-sacrificing, and concerned with duty.

Seven is the most significant and magical of the numbers. It is long been held sacred, and appears frequently in mythology and the Bible. There are seven notes in the musical scale, seven phases of the Moon, seven seas, seven heavenly bodies in the Ptolemaic system, and seven wonders of the world. The seventh son of a seventh son is believed to possess great magical powers. People who are Sevens are great thinkers and may have an occult or psychic side. They may be researchers, investigators, or inventors.

Eight comes under the influence of Saturn. Its people will achieve success, but not necessarily happiness. They may possess the drive and ability to lead, and thus receive material wealth and recognition, but they can often drive themselves too hard, repressing their feelings, and missing out on satisfying relationships.

If One symbolizes the beginning, Nine embraces all the previous numbers and symbolizes finality. Nine reproduces itself, as the digits of all multiples of 9 add up to 9. It is a mystical number, with many Biblical references: nine orders of angels, a nine days' wonder, nine points of the law, nine months of pregnancy, and so on. The influence of Mars makes Nines determined fighters, but also impulsive and possessive.

Islam and Sufism

Islam grew out of mystical revelations to its founder, the prophet Muhammad, who lived in Arabia in the seventh century. The word Islam means surrender, and its central goal is to abandon the self and personal ambition, and to embrace the divine will. This goal is taken to its spiritual extreme in the teachings and rituals of the Sufis – the mystical orders within Islam.

Islam means submission to, or having peace with, God. It is the newest of the three monotheistic faiths, and is the principal religion of much of Asia. Its salient feature is devotion to the Koran, believed to be the revelation of God to Muhammad, through which a consistent body of doctrine, rituals, and laws have emerged. This is supplemented by a rich collection of traditional teachings, the Sunna, collated during and immediately after Muhammad's lifetime.

The Sufis

Sufis were the ecstatic mystics of Islam, inspired by the "throne verses" and other mystical elements of the Koran. The Sufi movement began in Saudi Arabia, and spread to Persia and India, where elements of Hinduism are incorporated into the Sufi customs. At times, Sufis challenged orthodox Muslim authority and were regarded as heretical.

Sufism was so-named because its adherents wore wool

CRESCENT AND STAR

Below: After the Ottoman conquest of Constantinople (now Istanbul) this ancient Byzantine symbol was adopted as the flag of the new empire. It was later adopted by other Islamic nations.

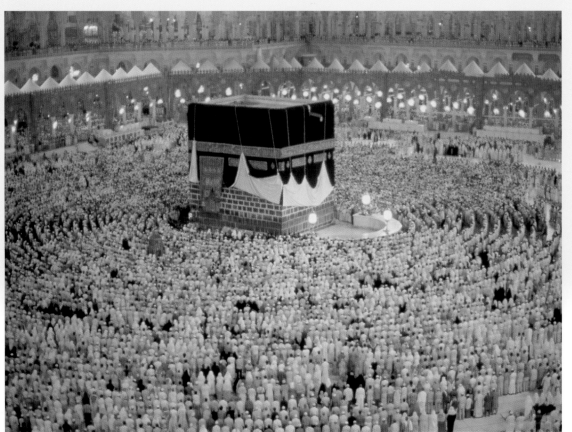

THE HAGIA SOFIA, ISTANBUL

Right: This vast Turkish mosque was a Byzantine church until the Ottoman conquest of 1453. Redecorated with glorious marbles and mosaic, it served as a template for many other mosques.

THE KAABA, MECCA

Left: Each year, thousands of Muslims make the Hajj (pilgrimage) to Mecca, the birthplace of Muhammad, and his tomb at Medina. The climax of the Mecca pilgrimage is visiting the Kaaba, which houses the sacred Black Stone. Pilgrims slowly circle the Kaaba seven times as part of their devotional ritual.

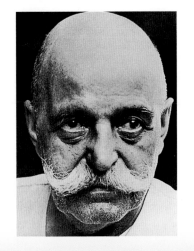

I knocked, and the door opened;
But I found that I had been
knocking from the inside.
Rumi, Sufi mystic and poet

garments like the early Christian ascetics (*suf*, meaning wool), and lived a life of devotion and prayer. They aimed to lose themselves in divine love through esoteric practices such as trance, meditation, and ecstatic dance and song.
Sufi ideology combined some elements from pre-Islamic shamanistic spirituality, Neo-Platonic philosophies of Ancient Greece, and other Islamic commentaries.

Sufi rituals

Sufism was organized into dervish orders, where members lived a life devoted to God and ritual. Rituals involved powerful verbal recitations proclaiming the devotees' belief in God, and vigorous dancing and breathing exercises, leading to personal hypnosis and transcendence expressing the union with God. Other dervish orders were less physical in their ritual, and concentrated on reciting confessionals of faith. The *shaykhs* who led the orders had complete authority over the members, and some were credited with magical and telepathic powers. A New Age Sufi revival is in progress worldwide, attracting both Muslims and non-Muslims. It applies the principles of the original Sufis through spiritual dance, poetry, and meditation.

The Enneagram

The enneagram is a graphic device used by specific Sufi orders for understanding human nature, and many of their theories fed back into Islamic mathematical literature. The Enneagram was introduced to the West in the 1920s by the mystic psychologist George Gurdjieff, famed for his personality theories. A later mystic, Oscar Ichazo, applied Gurdjieff's theories to the Enneagram, and it is this fusion of ideas which forms the basis of New Age Enneagram analysis. The Enneagram can be read in conjunction with other spiritual models, such as the Cabalistic Tree of Life developed by Jewish mystics.

DERVISH DANCE

The best-known image of Sufism is that of the whirling dervishes, whose spinning and jumping help them reach a state of spiritual unity with God. There were also howling dervishes who walked on, and swallowed, hot coals, without appearing to suffer.

Enneagram Analysis

Gurdjieff's theory states that there are nine major personality types and four main personality stages.

Stage One: Holy Idea. Each person is born with innate trust.

Stage Two: Fixation. As the child grows, they change to survive life's challenges, and this varies according to their particular weaknesses.

Stage Three: Passion. Each person develops a chief emotional trait for dealing with the loss of their childhood idyll.

Stage Four: Acquired Personality. Stage Three helps the individual navigate life, eventually confirming their set personality traits.

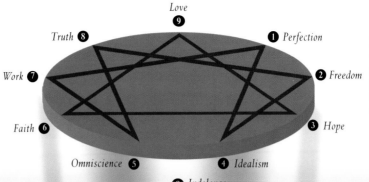

HOLY IDEA

These traits represent the essence of each personality type at birth, which is lost as one grows up.

Love 9 · Truth 8 · Perfection 1 · Freedom 2 · Work 7 · Faith 6 · Hope 3 · Omniscience 5 · Idealism 4

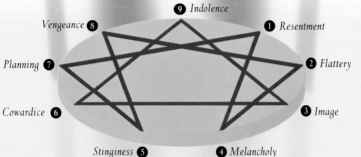

FIXATION

These traits are the mental images each personality forms to hide their fears and weaknesses, and to protect themselves as they get older.

Indolence 9 · Vengeance 8 · Resentment 1 · Planning 7 · Flattery 2 · Cowardice 6 · Image 3 · Stinginess 5 · Melancholy 4

INFLUENCES

Each personality is affected by its neighboring numbers, or "wings,", although one wing will always dominate. This diagram shows that Ones are affected by Twos and Nines.

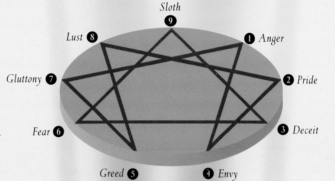

PASSION

These traits arise in each personality type to compensate for the loss of the Holy Idea.

Sloth 9 · Lust 8 · Anger 1 · Gluttony 7 · Pride 2 · Fear 6 · Deceit 3 · Greed 5 · Envy 4

INTERACTION

Each personality type interacts with one other, taking on some of their traits. In normal circumstances, Nines tends towards Sixes (red arrows). However, personalities lean to different types when feeling under stress (blue arrows) or safe and comfortable.

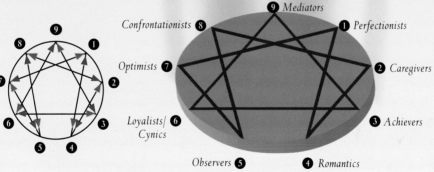

ACQUIRED PERSONALITY

These are the dominant characteristics of each personality type, once they have passed through stages one, two, and three.

Mediators 9 · Confrontationists 8 · Perfectionists 1 · Optimists 7 · Caregivers 2 · Loyalists/Cynics 6 · Achievers 3 · Observers 5 · Romantics 4

PERSONALITY TYPE

Gurdjieff's personality types were applied to the Enneagram by the later theorist, Ichazo.

1 Perfectionists who strive for excellence. Idealistic and conscientious, but can be angry and rigid.

2 Caregivers who look to others for endorsement. Empathetic, but always seeking approval and praise. Feel deflated if efforts are not valued.

3 Achievers and leaders who work hard for prestige. May sacrifice relationships to attain status. Avoid failure and defeat.

4 Romantics who are preoccupied with loss. Sensitive, moody, and artistic, they avoid the mundane.

5 Observers who view life from a distance. Detached and rational, they like analyzing the abstract. Greed keeps them from sharing.

6 Loyalists and Cynics. Find security in groups, yet suspicious of others' motives. The phobic Six is very cautious, while the counter-phobic Six rushes into situations too quickly.

7 Optimistic adventurers who are joyous and happy, but have trouble imposing personal limits.

8 Confrontationists and leaders with a lust for power. They respect those who stand up to them.

9 Easy-going and patient mediators. Not always self-starters, but high achievers once set on personal path.

Astrology

INFLUENCE OF THE STARS
Right: Scientific knowledge of
the solar system and the
earth's place in the universe
has made us question how
far celestial bodies affect
events – yet astrology is
increasingly popular.

Astrology is the ancient practice of predicting future events by studying the position and movements of the sun, moon, planets, and stars. It is one of the most popular ways in which individuals try to interpret their future.

Astrology was first developed in 600 B.C. by the Chaldeans and later the Assyrians, in southern Mesopotamia, in what is now Iraq. These advanced, city-building nations developed a system of divination based on astronomy (the scientific study of the movement of celestial bodies.) According to this first form of astrology the future of individuals and empires was predestined in the stars, not by the Gods. Decisions could not be made without interpreting the positions of the planets and stars.

Babylonian Astrology

The Babylonians were the first nation to interpret the stars using science, not the worship of sky gods. This form of astrology spread across Asia to the Mediterranean, where it was widely practiced by the classical Greeks and Romans. After Alexander the Great conquered Mesopotamia in 331 B.C., it became a widespread, secular activity, spreading into Europe.

Interest waned with the rise of Christianity, though astrology once again exerted a powerful influence during the Renaissance in Europe. Royalty and nobility even retained their own personal astrologers who were held in high esteem. However, in the sixteenth and seventeenth centuries the Church condemned the practice outright. As a result, astrology went into decline in Europe, although it remained popular in Arab lands. But astrology did not disappear altogether and today, although it has lost much of its importance, it is a democratic form of divination, available to everyone in the form of personal charts or horoscopes.

The Horoscope

The basic premise of astrological systems is that the universe is a unified whole in which all parts influence and affect each other. Ancient cultures were aware of this, but their knowledge faded over time. New Age science, such as New Physics, is now showing this old knowledge to be true.

The interpretation of astrology has shifted down the ages. The ancients believed that individuals' lives were predestined. Much later, astrology was viewed as a means of understanding

EARLY STUDY

Right: Astronomers all over the
world have been making
scientific studies of the stars as
far back as the fifteenth century.
Astrologers would use this
information when interpreting
peoples' horoscopes. This
illustration from the Babylonian
period shows astronomers using
sighting devices to chart the
position and movement of
celestial bodies. It is thought to
depict Caliph al-Mamun of
Baghdad.

THE 12 ZODIAC SIGNS

A system of symbols has evolved to represent the 12 zodiac constellations, or groups of stars. These are visible in the night sky, which is divided into the northern and southern hemispheres as shown here. In astrology, when the sun, moon, or planets pass through a constellation, it exerts the particular influence that is represented by its symbol.

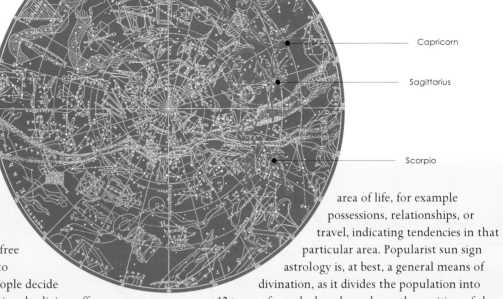

The Southern Hemisphere

Aquarius

Capricorn

Sagittarius

Scorpio

the self and changing influences on it. This enabled individuals to maximize their potential through the power of free will. This is the emphasis given to astrology in the New Age. As people decide that neither science nor conventional religion offers the answers to life's deepest questions, astrological readings offer a new way of approaching personal development and a reference point for developing the self. Like all other forms of divination, astrology is in essence a spiritual path.

Sun Sign Astrology

Sun sign astrology focuses on the movement and relative position of the stars and planets as they pass through the 12 zodiacs or houses of a person's horoscope. A person's sun sign depends on the day on which they were born – for example, a person born on October 13 is classified as a Libran. Each zodiac affects an area of life, for example possessions, relationships, or travel, indicating tendencies in that particular area. Popularist sun sign astrology is, at best, a general means of divination, as it divides the population into 12 types of people, based purely on the position of the sun at birth. Newspaper forecasts are based on this method, and can seem to ignore individual circumstances. However, a full astrological horoscope shows influences on an individual's life in more detail. It takes into account the individual's birth location, the planetary positions, and which house the planets occupy at the exact time of birth. A system of symbols has evolved to represent the 12 zodiac constellations. When the sun, moon, or any of the nine planets occupy a constellation, the latter exerts the particular influence represented by its symbol. The sign of Libra, for instance, is symbolized by the scales of justice, and influences issues of fairness and balance.

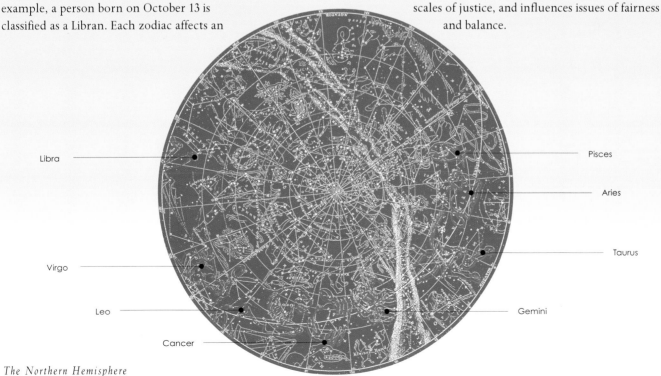

Libra

Virgo

Leo

Cancer

Pisces

Aries

Taurus

Gemini

The Northern Hemisphere

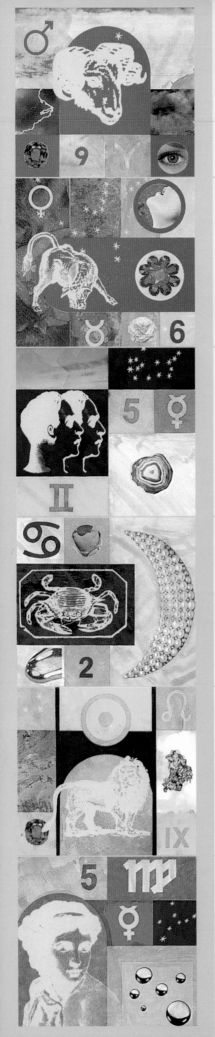

Aries
Symbol: Ram
Ruler: Mars
Sign: Fire
Positive: Aries people are innovative, impulsive, and adventurous. They like to lead and are very competitive.
Negative: Can be impatient, self-centered, or even aggressive when dealing with others.

Taurus
Symbol: Bull
Ruler: Venus
Sign: Earth
Positive: Taureans are steady, thorough, industrious, and patient. They are very grounded and enjoy the simple things in life.
Negative: Can be strong-willed or possessive and have a tendency to get stuck in a rut.

Gemini
Symbol: Twins
Ruler: Mercury
Sign: Air
Positive: Gemini people are quick, intelligent, and alert. They are adaptable and good communicators.
Negative: Can be restless, fickle, and changeable, and unable to finish projects that they start.

Cancer
Symbol: Crab
Ruler: Moon
Sign: Water
Positive: Cancerians are home-loving and family-oriented. They are sympathetic and nurturing and have a strong link to nature.
Negative: Can be secretive and defensive and may crave emotional security from others.

Leo
Symbol: Lion
Ruler: Sun
Sign: Fire
Positive: Leos are extroverts with strong leadership skills. They are also proud, brave, passionate, and full of life.
Negative: Can be overbearing, unchanging, and arrogant. They may even crave attention.

Virgo
Symbol: Maiden
Ruler: Mercury
Sign: Earth
Positive: Virgo people are skillful, methodical, efficient, and highly creative. They are committed to the service of humanity.
Negative: They can be over-critical perfectionists and are often plagued by self-doubt.

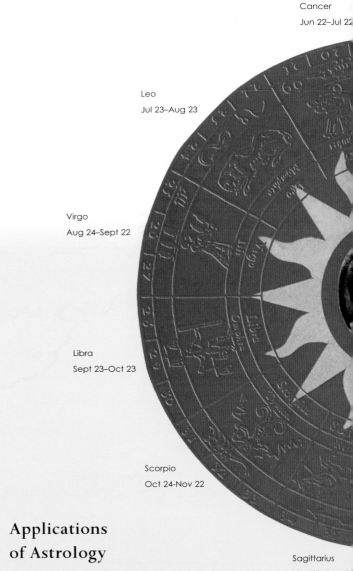

Cancer
Jun 22–Jul 22

Leo
Jul 23–Aug 23

Virgo
Aug 24–Sept 22

Libra
Sept 23–Oct 23

Scorpio
Oct 24–Nov 22

Sagittarius
Nov 23–Dec 2?

Applications of Astrology

A number of specialized forms of Western astrology have been developed for particular purposes:

Mundane astrology is concerned with global influences, for instance, those that might affect politics or natural disasters.

Horary astrology creates a chart for the precise moment of a specific event. It can be used, for instance, to choose an auspicious time to start a new venture or to get married.

Financial astrology focuses on economics and money, and is used in the financial centers of the world.

Psychological and counseling astrology focuses on the inner person, highlighting influences that could be connected to emotional illness, problems, crises, or turning points.

Medical astrology is based on the ancient belief that the 12 signs influence different parts of the body. Depending on what the individual birth chart reveals, this influence can either be a strength or a weakness. In the Middle Ages, medical astrology was used to diagnose illness, but is now used as a focus for contemplating one's physical self.

Gemini
May 22–Jun 21

Taurus
Apr 21–May 21

Aries
Mar 21–Apr 20

Pisces
Feb 19–Mar 20

Aquarius
Jan 21–Feb 18

Capricorn
Dec 22–Jan 18

Alchemic astrology follows the belief that the celestial bodies governed the growth of everything on earth, including metals. As the production of gold is the primary objective of alchemists, this relationship is vital to the quest for the Philosopher's Stone. New Age alchemists use the language and theories of the ancient astrologers as a springboard for analyzing the realms of psychology and philosophy.

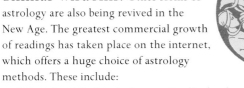

Similar wisdoms: Other forms of astrology are also being revived in the New Age. The greatest commercial growth of readings has taken place on the internet, which offers a huge choice of astrology methods. These include:

Sidereal and Vedic astrology originally developed in India and South East Asia.

Mayan astrology from Central America.

Chinese astrology systems, based on the cyclical patterns of the earth's energies.

Libra
Symbol: Scales
Ruler: Venus
Sign: Earth
Positive: Librans are thoughtful, rational, moderate, kind, and diplomatic. They strive for harmony and balance.
Negative: They have an inability to make decisions, and tend to compromise to avoid trouble.

Scorpio
Symbol: Scorpion
Ruler: Pluto
Sign: Water
Positive: Scorpions are secretive, mysterious, charismatic, intense, and full of passion. They are often thought to be psychic.
Negative: Can be difficult for others to deal with and may be unforgiving or vengeful.

Sagittarius
Symbol: Archer
Ruler: Jupiter
Sign: Fire
Positive: Sagittarians are honest and sincere. Life is an adventure to be explored and they are optimistic and enjoy challenges.
Negative: Can be outspoken, tactless, and impulsive, and may take unnecessary personal risks.

Capricorn
Symbol: Goat
Ruler: Saturn
Sign: Earth
Positive: Capricorns are honest, stable, and conventional. They are reserved but quietly tenacious and patient.
Negative: Can be pessimistic, mean, and unwilling to experiment.

Aquarius
Symbol: Water bearer
Ruler: Uranus
Sign: Air
Positive: Aquarians are independent spirits who dislike convention. They are idealist and humanitarian, with a desire to make the world a better place.
Negative: Can reject valuable advice because it is conventional.

Pisces
Symbol: Fishes
Ruler: Neptune
Sign: Water
Positive: Pisceans are gentle, loving, and compassionate. They are dreamy, romantic, intuitive, and spiritual.
Negative: Can be too vague, passive, sentimental, and easily led for their own good.

AFRICA AND EGYPT

The long and complex history of the second-largest continent is shrouded in mystery and still only partly known. Home to man's oldest ancestor, and birthplace of the ancient Egyptian civilization, much of Africa remained impenetrable and unexplored by the outside world until relatively recently. This isolation has resulted in the conservation of age-old traditions, while at the same time written history is frustratingly patchy, with centuries-long gaps in our knowledge of events. A significant number of New Age practices can trace their origins back to Africa, including astrology, aromatherapy, color healing, herbalism, and the use of crystals, as well as some of the oldest forms of magic and divination.

Africa

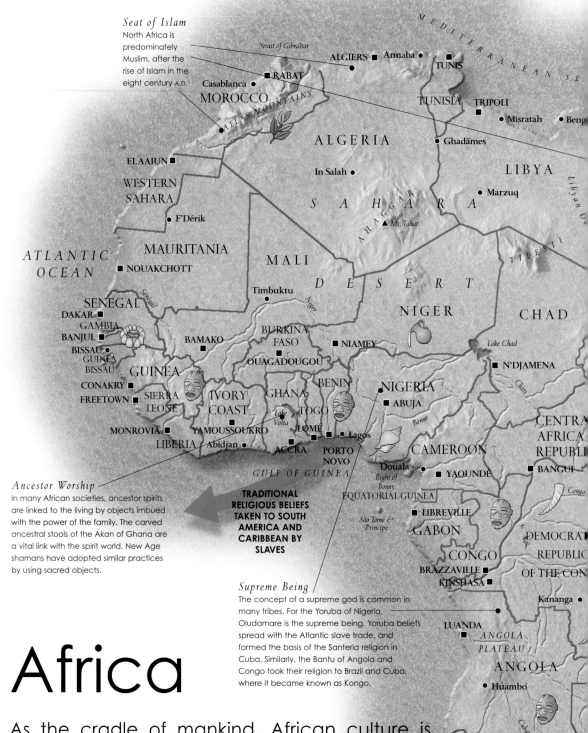

TIME LINE

4.2 million years B.C.
Man's oldest ancestor, Hominid species (*Australopithecus afarensis*) inhabits Ethiopia.

1.8 million years B.C.
Evidence of *Homo habilis* inhabiting areas of Tanzania and Kenya.

1 million years B.C.
Homo erectus migrates to Europe and Asia.

10,000–6,000 B.C.
Farming society develops.

2000 B.C.
Egyptian society adopts solar calendar.

300–400 B.C.
Bantu tribes displace the San in South Africa.

100s A.D.
Malay-Polynesians migrate from Asia to Madagascar.

400–600s
Christianity and Islam spread through Egypt and Ethiopia.

1100–1500s
Swahili move along East coast, adopting Indian and Arab traditions.

c. 1100–1897
Rise of Benin Kingdom. Development of voodoo (or vodou) belief system.

1498
Vasco da Gama arrives in Mombasa in search of a sea route to India.

c. 1597
Joao dos Santos records Bantu culture in *Ethiopia Oriental*.

1600s
Golden age of African Islam, with Timbuktu as center of learning.

1807
Great Britain outlaws Atlantic slave trade.

1870–1960
European colonialism breaks up tribal culture. Christian missionaries convert millions.

1990s
Islam remains dominant in North Africa, and tribal beliefs continue in central and southern regions. Voodoo, Santeria, and Kongo continue in the Caribbean and South America.

Seat of Islam
North Africa is predominately Muslim, after the rise of Islam in the eight century A.D.

Ancestor Worship
In many African societies, ancestor spirits are linked to the living by objects imbued with the power of the family. The carved ancestral stools of the Akan of Ghana are a vital link with the spirit world. New Age shamans have adopted similar practices by using sacred objects.

TRADITIONAL RELIGIOUS BELIEFS TAKEN TO SOUTH AMERICA AND CARIBBEAN BY SLAVES

Supreme Being
The concept of a supreme god is common in many tribes. For the Yoruba of Nigeria, Oludamare is the supreme being. Yoruba beliefs spread with the Atlantic slave trade, and formed the basis of the Santeria religion in Cuba. Similarly, the Bantu of Angola and Congo took their religion to Brazil and Cuba, where it became known as Kongo.

As the cradle of mankind, African culture is arguably the oldest on earth. Many tribal traditions remain intact, and have spread across the globe through migration, both voluntary and forced. The Ancient Egyptian civilization had its own unique cultural mix, and was the origin of many of the disciplines now established in the New Age Movement.

Mystic Energies
Table Mountain is a popular New Age pilgrimage for travelers who come to bathe in the mystic energies that run across ley lines over the mountain.

Sacred stone circles

Sacred water of the River Niger

Traditional religious beliefs, such as voodoo

Yoruba shell divination

Practice of herbal medicine

Formal musical traditions

Ancient Christian communities

Sacred Mount Kenya

Sacred Table Mountain

Alexandria

CAIRO • Suez

Nile

RED SEA

EGYPT

Aswan •

Lake Nasser

Wadi-Halfa •

Nubian Desert

Port Sudan •

N

KHARTOUM ■

Kassala •

ERITREA

■ ASMERA

Wad Medani •

Blue Nile

Gulf of Aden

DJIBOUTI
■ DJIBOUTI

SUDAN

■ ADDIS ABABA

SOMALIA

ETHIOPIAN HIGHLANDS

White Nile

ETHIOPIA

Ancient Christians
Ethiopia and Sudan have the oldest Christian community in Africa

UGANDA

KENYA

MOGADISHU ■

Margherita Peak ▲

KAMPALA ■

Mt. Kenya ▲

ARAB SETTLERS ARRIVE FROM THE EIGHTH CENTURY A.D., INFLUENCING NATIVE SWAHILI CULTURE

RWANDA
KIGALI ■

Lake Victoria

■ NAIROBI

Tana

■ BUJUMBURA

Kilimanjaro ▲

BURUNDI

• Mombasa

Zanzibar

Lake Tanganyika

DODOMA ■

Rufiji

• Dar-es-Salaam

Lake Mweru

TANZANIA

Lake Nyasa

MALAWI

ZAMBIA

■ LILONGWE

Moçambique •

LUSAKA •

• Blantyre

Harare

Zambezi

ANTANANARIVO ■

ZIMBABWE

• Beira

Bulawayo •

MADAGASCAR

MOZAMBIQUE

Limpopo

MALAY-POLYNESIAN MIGRANTS SETTLE FROM THE SIXTH CENTURY A.D.

PRETORIA

■ MAPUTO
■ MBABANE

SWAZILAND

MASERU

LESOTHO

Africa is generally regarded as the birthplace of humanity itself; there is evidence that man first started walking upright on this continent at least four million years ago. True humans, who made and used tools, appeared some millions of years later. Their remains have been found in the Great Rift Valley and in caves in Southern Africa.

By 120,000 B.C., a hunter-gatherer lifestyle was established. Ceremonial burial sites indicate that spiritual activity had begun by the Middle Stone Age, around 42,000 years ago. Rock paintings from the Sahara desert, dating from 10,000 B.C., depict tribespeople with the supernatural beings that they revered. This culture survived through the Bush People of the Kalahari.

Over the subsequent eras, hunter-gathering gave way to shifting cultivation, then to pastoralism, but the shamanistic patterns of spirituality survived. Even though African society is universally organized along tribal lines, indigenous beliefs have much in common across the continent. When Africa was divided into colonial territories in the nineteenth century, Christianity was introduced into many areas and elements of native culture became integrated into the new faith. Northern and eastern regions of the continent are mainly Islamic.

Spirituality permeated every element of daily life in Africa. The world of nature contained many spirit beings and powers, and ancestors also played a key role in cultural traditions. These all exerted influence on humans, who could intercede with them. This type of shamanism included the use of mediums and divination, both of which are still common in sub-Saharan Africa.

African magic

Magic is the attempt to influence human experience using more than purely physical measures, and Africa is regarded by many as its birthplace. Early magical rituals contained the beginnings of mythology, astronomy, medicine, and psychology, and also religion.

PROTECTIVE CLOTHING
Amulets and coins, like those worn by this Samburu dancer from Kenya, are thought to ward off evil, sickness, or other misfortunes.

The first applications of magic related to the hunt, the ancestors, and the mother goddess. As society developed, the focus shifted to other important concerns, such as crop fertility and the health of animal herds. In the West, magic eventually became divorced from everyday life, and more intellectual in content. Although religious authorities would often persecute its practitioners, it has always been maintained by secret societies such as the alchemists, Freemasons, Rosicrucians, and Templars.

The great forces of nature and the universe have always been believed to affect humans through the phenomena of birth, death, sickness, hunger, and so on. The New Age approach to magic is based on this ancient recognition. Magic, therefore, may not follow the laws of modern science, but it does obey the laws of the universe.

Talismans

A talisman is an object imbued with special energies or powers that are believed to bring health, success, or good fortune to its possessor. It is one of the oldest forms of magical object. Talismans were first discovered in ancient Ethiopia, and have been widely used in Africa right up to the present day.

Talismans often have a specific purpose, such as to influence the outcome of a journey or a dangerous undertaking. They are made from natural objects that possess particular qualities, and these qualities are then further strengthened by ritual or ceremony. The objects might be parts of totemic animals, such as the foot of a rabbit or the claw of a bird, a snakeskin, or a precious stone. Coins and holy relics are also used in this way.

Amulets

Amulets do not possess the active power of talismans. Nevertheless, they are still thought able to provide protection against disease or other misfortune. Amulets include precious stones, figures of deities or saints, and natural items such as flowers, seeds, or nuts.

HERD MENTALITY
Below: Wildebeest of the Kalahari and other creatures that were hunted for meat became an early focus of magic, reflecting man's concern for the health of the herds.

THE MAGIC CONTINENT
Right: This prehistoric petroglyph of a man and a giraffe was discovered in Algeria, and underlines the claim of the African continent to be the cradle of magic.

Similar wisdoms: African talismans and amulets have many equivalents in other parts of the world. These include shamanistic charms, aboriginal totems, Native American fetishes, Chinese household amulets, Islamic basmallahs and Greek abrax stones. In medieval Europe, rubies were used as amulets to give protection against the plague.

African oracles

Systems of divination have existed in Africa longer than on any other continent. Many go right back to the Stone Age, yet are still widely practiced today. Methods include bone divination, Ifa, a Yoruba practice, and geomancy, which involves the interpretation of marks made in sand or earth.

RIDDLE OF THE SANDS

In Mali, West Africa, experts believe they can foretell the future from the tracks left overnight by wandering foxes.

The use of the bone oracle is the oldest and most basic system of divination known to humankind. It is also the most widespread: it has been used all over the world, from the Neolithic period right up to the present day. In Africa, it is thought to have originated in the ancient kingdom of Zimbabwe, spreading outward from there through tribal migration and trade. It is still extremely popular today, even in modern urban areas.

The bones used in the oracle can be made from real animal bone, or from horn, ivory, or shell. They are uniquely connected to their owner, and empowered by ritual. Their power is based on the close connection between human and animal energy in the spirit world. Each bone has two facets, one negative and one positive.

There are two main systems. One uses a set of four bones, ranked in importance. The other uses an array of up to sixty small bones, which may also include special stones. In both systems the diviner throws the bones, then interprets their message—which might relate to a present problem, or indicate future events—according to the way they fall. Interpretations are based on the social and cultural order, and in turn reflect levels of order in the natural world and in the cosmos. The diviner will have learned the whole range of meanings given by different combinations of the bones, and during the reading he recites them in the form of verses known as praises. This is followed by a more specific interpretation of the issue in hand.

Like most African spiritual practitioners, the diviners pass on their knowledge from generation to generation within the family. Many are also doctors and herbalists, using the bones for the diagnosis and treatment of illness.

Similar wisdoms:

The bone oracle has a number of parallels. The Nordic runes and the Chinese I Ching, for example, also use the casting of objects to produce standardized verses of interpretation.

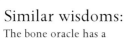

READING THE AUGURIES

A world of meaning is read into the pattern of bones and other ritual items scattered randomly on this Yoruba divination plate (left) from Nigeria.

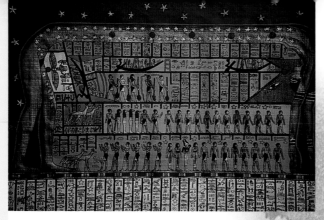

By marking the rise of the floodwaters of the Nile, the Ancient Egyptians developed their knowledge of astronomy, noticing that the rise and fall of the river coincided with certain positions of the moon and stars. Above: Nut, Goddess of the Sky, supports the heavens and protects sailors on the river.

KEY

Bedouin nomadic culture

Coptic monastery

Oasis

Temple/ancient site

Mediterranea

INFLUX OF ANCIENT GREEK CULT

Al Bardi
Umm Sa'ad
Sidi Barrani
Marsa Matruh
El 'Alamein

Lybian Plateau

Qattara Depression

Wadi an-Natrun

Siwa

LIBYA

Libyan Desert

EGYPT

P
El

Far
Oa

Qasr Far

Weste

Dese

El Qas
N

Egypt

A melting pot for a host of spiritual beliefs, Ancient Egypt has been studied more than any other society. The Egyptians were masters of crystal work, healing with color and light, aromatherapy, and mysticism and magic, all of which play a significant role in the New Age.

The scarab beetle was a popular Egyptian symbol of rebirth and good fortune, often appearing as decoration on elaborate tombs.

Gilf Kebir Plateau

Al Uwaynat

Myrrh was a vital ingredient for incense and in embalming. Today this ancient wisdom is the basis for the use of essential oils in aromatherapy. Hatshepsut, the only female Pharaoh, is said to have personally visited the land of Punt (present-day Somalia) to bring back myrrh for her temple at Deir el-Bahri.

SUDA

Alexandria, founded in 332 B.C. This cultured, cosmopolitan city was well known all over the world for its library and scholars of science and alchemy.

Mount Sinai is considered sacred because it is said to be where Moses received the Ten Commandments.

N

ea

ISRAEL

Dumyat
ashid
xandria   El Mansura   Port Said   El'Arish
  Disuq
nanhur   Samanud
  Tanta
Zagazig
  Isma'iliya
Benha   Heliopolis
El Giza   CAIRO   Suez
ZA
  Sudr
aiyum

Nile

Gulf of Suez

Sinai

Elat
Taba

Nuweiba

Suef   ST. ANTHONY
m Ombo—home   Mt. Sinai
the Egyptian   ST. PAUL
ocodile god, Sebek.   ST. CATHERINE   Dahab   SAUDI
  Ras Gharib   ARABIA
El Minya   El Tur
MUN   Sharm el Shiek   Na'ama

ARRIVAL
OF ISLAM
IN THE SIXTH
CENTURY
A.D.

AKHETATEN   Hurghada

Asyut

Nile

Sohag   Bur Safaga

Eastern Desert

Qena   Quseir
ABYDOS   DENDARA
  Karnak
NAG HAMMADI   Luxor
arga   Armant

Red Sea

Isna   DEIR EL-BAHRI

Great   Idfu   Marsa Alam
Oasis

Nile

Kom Ombo

PHILAE   Birenice
Aswan Dam   Aswan

Bir Shalatein

Lake
Nasser

Abu Simbel

Wadi Halfa

Nubian
Desert

Egyptian civilization has always centered on the valley of the great River Nile, which is closely hemmed in by desert. In the hot, dry climate, the river provides irrigation and transport, and seasonal flooding deposits alluvial nutrients, invaluable for agriculture. The deserts that flank the valley are rich in metals, precious stones such as turquoise and quartz, and stone for building. They also provide a considerable degree of security against attack.

Civilization in Egypt goes back a very long way. At the end of the last Ice Age, around 10,000 years ago, the valley was populated by hunter-gatherers. At around 6000 B.C., Neolithic farming villages appeared along the river. A unified kingdom was formed as early as 3200 B.C., and was ruled by a succession of Pharaoh dynasties that lasted nearly 3,000 years. This was a time of rapid advances in craftsmanship and technology; the great pyramid at El Giza was constructed around 2,600 B.C. Egyptian power was at its greatest between 1600 and 1000 B.C., before the New Kingdom went into decline, leading ultimately to the first of many invasions that culminated in the Arab conquest in the seventh century A.D.

Egyptian Spirituality

Early Egyptian spirituality began with shamanistic worship of the natural world, focusing particularly on totemic animals. In Egyptian mythology, these were identified as the ancestors of human clans. When Egyptian culture was at its height, they evolved into hybridized human and animal deities, many having human bodies with animal heads. Horus, the falcon-headed sky god, is one example.

Mythology was also rooted in Egypt's main environmental influences – the river Nile and the sun. The sun was the archetypal symbol of light triumphing over darkness, and good overcoming evil. The river, with its annual cycles of drought and flooding, was equated with the process of life, death, and rebirth.

From the time of the Napoleonic expeditions onward, and particularly after the decoding of hieroglyphics from the Rosetta stone, Egyptology became an established science. This led to a series of major archaeological ventures in the nineteenth and early twentieth centuries. In 1922, the tomb of Tutankhamen was discovered, with all its treasures intact. Some believe that the series of calamities that subsequently befell its investigators arose from this intrusion.

Since ancient times, there has been much speculation about the existence of an even older Egyptian civilization, dating from before most of the country became desert.

Magic and mysticism

Egyptian mysticism has profoundly influenced spiritual traditions in both East and West. Indeed, Egyptian culture has long had a reputation for holding the key to lost secrets. As one of the oldest civilisations of which historical records still survive, it continues to exert its fascination on followers of the New Age.

It was claimed that Egyptian practitioners could foretell the future with great accuracy. Perhaps the most distinctive method for doing this was through hieroglyphic magic, a sacred form of symbolic writing in which the hieroglyphs themselves contained powerful energies. According to this, the Scarab could affect rebirth, and the Eye of Horus evoke the power of the sun.

The Egyptians had a strong belief in life after death, which provided an important focus in funeral ritual for the country's elite. Immortality was secured for the Pharaohs by mummification and elaborate burial; next to the body was placed the Book of the Dead, a collection of papyruses containing charms and spells to guide them to the afterworld.

The Pyramids

The Egyptian pyramids are among the largest and most enigmatic structures ever created by humankind. No existing documents explain why they were built. Conventionally, they have always been regarded merely as elaborate burial chambers; curiously, however, no bodies have ever been found in them. Arab writers in the early Middle Ages considered them to be repositories of secret wisdom and lost scientific knowledge, acquired by the Egyptians from earlier, unknown civilizations. It has also been suggested that the shape itself was designed to generate energy, or that the pyramids provided a kind of launch pad for astral projection.

The period during which the pyramids were built is known as the Old Kingdom, lasting from 2700 B.C. to 2200 B.C. The first known example of a pyramid was a stepped structure, 200 ft (62m) high, built around 2650 B.C. The true pyramid shape evolved from this prototype, under the instructions of the Temple of the Sun priesthood at Heliopolis.

The Great Pyramid at Giza, built for King Cheops in 2600 B.C., is the largest stone building ever created, ancient or modern. It is 482 ft (147m) high and is made of 2.3 million blocks that weigh up to 70 tons apiece. It was constructed with almost unbelievable accuracy, with tolerances down to one hundredth of an inch (0.2mm). Some authorities believe it may have been constructed by using sonics – the power of ultrasound, harnessed at very specific frequencies, but no one can guess how the ancient Egyptians might have acquired this technology.

HIEROGLYPHICS

Hieroglyphics and relief carvings (far left) have provided insights into the belief systems of the Egyptians. Magicians and soothsayers occupied an important place in society in ancient Egypt, and many of their secrets are still to be discovered.

CULTURAL LOGOS

Above and left: The left eye of the falcon god Horus was said to be the protective symbol of the moon. The scarab, or sacred beetle, was dedicated to Ra, the sun god, as its habit of rolling its ball of dung ahead of it was taken to represent the daily journey of the sun across the sky. It has featured in ornamentation down the ages.

SYMBOL OF INSCRUTABILITY

Right: The Sphinx, so named by Greek historian Herodotus, has the head of a man and the body of a lion. It stands near the three pyramids at Giza.

Similar wisdoms:

The Book of the Dead has been closely echoed in other cultures. The Tibetan *Book of the Dead* is one example.

The power of crystals

Crystals and gemstones embody the age-old power of the earth, and it was ancient Egyptian alchemists and magicians who first used them in a systematic way for healing, transformation, and spiritual enhancement. This inherent power, rather than their esthetics, provided the real reason why precious stones were valued. It also helps to explain why they appear in the crowns of monarchs, as in most cases temporal leaders were originally spiritual leaders.

SPIRITUAL AND TEMPORAL POWER

Above: Crystals and gems, such as turquoise, had to be carefully prized from the surrounding rock in which they were formed, then fashioned into decorative shapes for setting in jewelry.

Left: Ramses II ruled for sixty-seven years from around 1300 B.C. He was one of a long line of Egyptian rulers whose power was believed to radiate from their bejeweled head-dresses. Most of the Egyptian statues from this period were carved from tough igneous quartz porphyry.

The Egyptians especially favored the use of quartz, which for them represented the Eye of Horus. They also used turquoise, which gave protection against negative influences, and lapis lazuli, which symbolized the energies of the heart.

Crystals have, however, been used since prehistoric times. In shamanistic cultures, from the Tlingit Eskimos to the Amazon Conibo, quartz is still the most highly regarded crystal. This is because shamanism perceives that everything has an outer, worldly image as well as a different inner or spiritual image. Crystalline quartz is one of the few minerals to display its inner structure on its external surfaces: it is therefore seen to connect heaven and earth, and is ascribed unique magical powers.

Stones with a crystalline structure have special electrical properties. Some crystals are transmitters, sending out positive and useful energies, while others are receivers, absorbing negative energies, such as pain in the body. The high ratios of mica or quartz contained in the stones used to build ancient megalithic constructions is believed to be one of the reasons why these sites generate special energies. In the 1960s, Russian scientists postulated that the earth itself might have an immense crystalline structure at its core, creating magnetic fields and volcanic activity, and influencing bird migration and the siting of ancient civilizations. There is a theory that the inhabitants of the lost city of Atlantis used crystals to generate energy for running machinery, and that it was abuse of this resource that led to the downfall of the whole of its civilization.

In the New Age, crystals are once again widely used, and many people now have their own personal gems. These may be worn or carried, or applied in specific ways; they are also used in electrocrystal therapy. Gem elixirs can be made by leaving crystals in water. Specific applications range from protection, healing, and empowerment, to divination, fortune-telling, and psychic work.

Recently, a series of ancient artifacts called the Crystal Skulls has been discovered. The skulls come from different sources all over the world. Some believe that their powerful energies play an important role in the survival and evolution of human life.

The use of crystals is closely integrated with studies of light, color, and the subtle energies of the human body, which are described next.

Similar wisdoms: In Australian aboriginal culture, quartz is thought of as solidified light and energy, and is used a great deal in shamanistic initiation. Native Americans are traditionally given a personal stone at birth, which is carried in a pouch at all times.

Power from color and light

From earliest times, color has been of vital significance in matters of rite and ritual, nowhere more so than in Egypt as evidenced in the lavish decoration of its rulers' tombs. As humankind evolved from hunting to farming, the ritualistic use of color broadened.

There is a theory that color healing originated in Atlantis, and was taken from there to Egypt, where it was developed to a high degree. The Egyptians had healing centers throughout the land, in the form of specially constructed temples that channeled sunlight in controlled beams. The name of their most holy city, Heliopolis, means city of the sun. In India, healer-priests had their own system of color science, while in medieval Europe Paracelsus formulated a methodology for using colors for healing. Until the New Age revival, however, color healing had fallen into disuse, and was a more or less forgotten art.

The seven major colors are formed when sunlight is broken down into different wavelengths. Ancient Egyptians, like other peoples, were aware of the essentially sevenfold nature of color; modern science is confirming what they already knew. The color blue, for instance, calms the nerves, steadies breathing, and lowers blood pressure. Red, by contrast, excites the nervous system, increases metabolic rate, and raises blood pressure. Pink can reduce aggression, and orange assists the digestion. In most ancient cultures, color was used in physical

MOOD X-RAYS
The gas discharge visualization machine, invented by a Russian scientist, photographs the human energy field using electronic and optic technology.

healing and spiritual rituals. in common with Tibetans, Native Americans, and others, the Egyptians regarded turquoise as the most sacred color, and used it as a symbol of heaven.

Today, color therapy often involves the human aura – a shimmering light surrounding the body that can be seen by practitioners – and the internal energy centers known as chakras (see opposite). Colors can sometimes be seen in the aura, indicating certain conditions. Yellow, for instance, indicates the capacity for communication. The chakras relate to certain color vibrations and these correspond to different organs or glands.

NEW LIGHT ON FORGOTTEN ART
Egypt had color healing centers, in the form of temples that channeled sunlight in controlled beams.

THE SEVEN CHAKRAS

Each chakra absorbs a different color into one of the main nerve centers of the body. The relationships are shown in descending order in the lefthand column below, together with corresponding minerals (center column) and their potential influence on the emotions (righthand column).

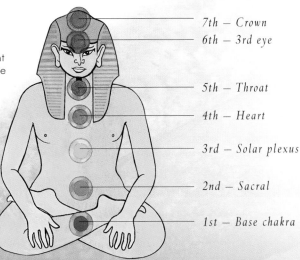

7th — Crown
6th — 3rd eye
5th — Throat
4th — Heart
3rd — Solar plexus
2nd — Sacral
1st — Base chakra

VIOLET

Crown – pineal gland, brain, and central nervous system.

CORRESPONDING MINERAL

Amethyst – treats emotional symptoms and ailments from blood impurities. It is energizing and helps break old behavior patterns.

INFLUENCE ON EMOTIONS

Violet is the color of transformation. It can exert strong psychic influences.

INDIGO

Third eye – pituitary gland, eyes, nose, ears, and skeletal system.

Sodalite, amethyst – indigo clears the head, is a strong sedative, and regenerates cells.

Indigo is associated with the right side of the brain and stimulates the imagination.

BLUE

Throat – thyroid gland, upper lungs, and respiratory system.

Sapphire, aquamarine, turquoise, lapis lazuli – blue inspires clarity and idealism. Sapphire treats insomnia and engenders compassion for others. Aquamarine aids physical and mental balance.

Blue inspires mental control, creativity, and clarity. Light blue gives a sense of security.

GREEN

Heart – thymus gland, lower lung, circulatory system, and parasympathetic nervous system.

Emerald, jade, tourmaline, moss agate – emerald treats weak digestion, colic, and skin problems. Jade treats kidneys, bladder, and eyes, and promotes clear thinking.

Green promotes empathy with others, and can be used to combat jealousy and possessiveness.

YELLOW

Solar plexus – pancreas, liver, gall bladder, spleen, digestive system, and nervous system.

Topaz, citrine, yellow zircon – topaz treats asthma, laryngitis, fever, exhaustion, and nervous trauma. Citrine promotes playfulness.

Yellow is uplifting and associated with the intellect and power of self-expression.

ORANGE

Sacral – reproductive organs, stomach, and colon.

Amber, topaz – amber treats rheumatism, asthma, intestinal disorders, and depression, and balances the endocrine system.

Orange aids sexual potency, boosts the immune system, and can counter alcoholism.

RED

Base – adrenals, kidneys, muscles, and arterial blood.

Ruby, garnet, agate, carnelian, coral, rose quartz – red stones treat heart disease, circulatory problems, anemia, and eye disease. Coral treats hemorrhoids and sexual diseases, and aids meditation. Rose quartz promotes friendship.

Red stimulates vitality and ambition. It can help overcome negative thoughts, but is also associated with anger.

The art of aromatherapy

The priestly classes and nobility of ancient Egypt used concentrated plant oils for religious, cosmetic, and medicinal purposes. Laboratories within the ancient temples kept detailed records of how the oils should be administered, and many of the same methods are still used by modern-day aromatherapists. The term aromatherapy was coined by René-Maurice Gattefosse, a French chemist who was at the forefront of 20th century research into essential oils.

We know so much about the ancient Egyptians' use of aromatherapy because their priests went to great lengths to keep detailed records of their work, recording their recipes on papyrus scrolls or stone tablets and thus ensuring that their knowledge was passed on to later generations and other scientific cultures, such as the Assyrians and Babylonians. Each temple would have its own laboratory for the study of plants,

BURIED TREASURE

Above and left: Ancient Egyptian nobility were dedicated users of aromatic oils and perfumed materials. They were also buried with aromatic preparations, kept in alabaster stone jars. When Tutankamen's tomb was uncovered, a fragrant odor still persisted from the original ointments stored in jars for thousands of years.

HATSHEPSUT'S HERBAL GARDEN

Right: Hatshepsut, the female Pharaoh from circa 1500 B.C., was famed for her collection of wild frankincense, myrrh, and balsam, which she planted in the temple garden at Deir el Bahri. A red mound of myrrh remains on the temple wall as a reminder of the expedition.

Balsam

Frankincense

Myrrh

SCENTED MUSIC

Ancient Egyptian musicians wore cones of scented grease and perfumed herbs. The Egyptians imported specialist herbs, oils, and spices from the Indian sub-continent to supplement their own locally grown supply. Paintings on tombs and temples depict the use of oils and fragrance in domestic scenes.

and the use of essential oils is woven into the ancient legends of Egyptian religion. They even worshipped their own fragrance deity, Nefertem, who is depicted on tombs and temples rising out of the lotus flower. As in other folk cultures, tribal healers also used plants and herbs to heal the sick. Essential oils were extracted by steeping the plants in cold fats, macerating them in hot oil, or pressing them to extract the aromatic elements. Plants were also used dried, like modern pot pourri, or dried and ground to form a perfumed powder. Physicians used herbs, essential oils, resins, and spices for medicated baths, poultices, and for massage – very much as they are used today.

Aromatherapy Today

Essential oils are easily inhaled or absorbed through the skin, where their medicinal properties are allowed to enter the bloodstream. The extraction of oils is expensive, with huge quantities of plant stock required for a small quantity of oil. The oils have differing physical and psychological benefits, including antiseptic, warming, cooling, astringent, stimulating, soothing, relaxing, sedative, decongestant, and antispasmodic properties. As the oils are highly concentrated and extremely powerful, caution must be observed when self-administering, especially when pregnant.

The professional aromatherapist is usually trained in massage, as this is the most common method of administering the oils. In a typical consultation, the practitioner would take a full medical history, together with details of the specific symptoms to be treated. A mix of oils is prepared and the patient is asked if they like the smell before use. The prescribed oil is then transferred to a neutral or carrier massage oil and applied directly to the skin. Alternatively it may be warmed in an aromatherapy burner so that the oil evaporates into the air, or a few drops may be added to hot bathwater.

Marigold

Sage

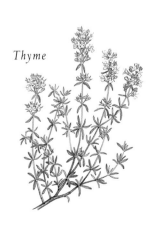

Thyme

AROMATHERAPY TODAY

Using modern cultivation methods, there are about 40 widely used essential oils made from aromatic plants. Many garden herbs, such as sage and thyme, offer medicinal benefits, and the professional aromatherapist usually combines a mixture of oils in a neutral carrier oil to treat specific symptoms.

INDIA

From the viewpoint of spiritual traditions, the subcontinent of India includes not only Pakistan and Bangladesh, but also the Himalayan lands of Nepal, Bhutan, and Tibet. This great and populous landmass has nurtured an ancient and distinctive culture, the source of many of the world's belief systems as well as New Age practices.

India

The spiritual traditions of the Indian sub-continent are dominated by Hinduism, Sikhism, and Islam, all of which have provided a rich source of inspirational material for New Age practitioners.

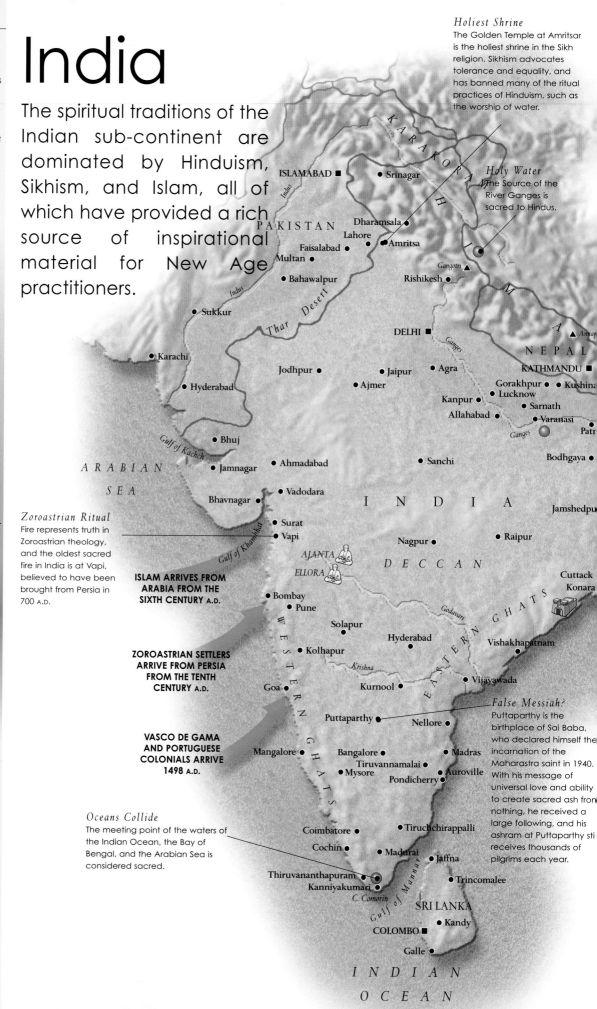

Holiest Shrine
The Golden Temple at Amritsar is the holiest shrine in the Sikh religion. Sikhism advocates tolerance and equality, and has banned many of the ritual practices of Hinduism, such as the worship of water.

Holy Water
The Source of the River Ganges is sacred to Hindus.

Zoroastrian Ritual
Fire represents truth in Zoroastrian theology, and the oldest sacred fire in India is at Vapi, believed to have been brought from Persia in 700 A.D.

ISLAM ARRIVES FROM ARABIA FROM THE SIXTH CENTURY A.D.

ZOROASTRIAN SETTLERS ARRIVE FROM PERSIA FROM THE TENTH CENTURY A.D.

VASCO DE GAMA AND PORTUGUESE COLONIALS ARRIVE 1498 A.D.

Oceans Collide
The meeting point of the waters of the Indian Ocean, the Bay of Bengal, and the Arabian Sea is considered sacred.

False Messiah?
Puttaparthy is the birthplace of Sai Baba, who declared himself the incarnation of the Maharastra saint in 1940. With his message of universal love and ability to create sacred ash from nothing, he received a large following, and his ashram at Puttaparthy sti receives thousands of pilgrims each year.

KEY

Buddhist caves

Konarak temple built in honor of Surya

Sites of sacred water worship

Winter Celebration
Hindu pilgrims celebrate the winter solstice at Sagar Dwip where the Ganges meets the ocean.

Varanasi
Varanasi has been India's holiest city since 1500 B.C. Situated on the River Ganges, its waters are said to relieve Hindus from the cycle of rebirth, while dying in the river leads to immediate enlightenment.

Since the 1960s, Indian culture has been at the center of New Age understanding. A great number of spiritual and physical disciplines have been exported, converting the West to new world views and offering new ways to self-knowledge and self-improvement.

Spirituality within India is not confined to ancient history. There are many modern pilgrimages that symbolize the ever-evolving religious experiences of Indians and visitors. The City of Dawn, or Auroville, was set up in 1968 to promote universal harmony. It was led by The Mother, successor to Sri Aurobindo, a well-known spiritual healer. The planned city for up to 50,000 residents still exists, and aims to bring together men and women of different creeds. Central to the community is the Matrimandir, a giant meditation dome.

Other modern spiritual movements include the Self-Realization Fellowship. It was founded by Paramahansa Yogananda, born in Gorakhpur on the Nepalese border. He lectured widely abroad and attracted several well-known students such as George Eastman and Leopold Stokowski. His 1946 *Autobiography of a Yogi* is a classic.

Pune is the home of the Osho Commune International, founded by the controversial guru Bhagwan Sri Rajneesh. In spite of his deportation from the United States in 1985, and his death in 1990, the commune's mix of Indian mysticism, Californian psychology, and sexual liberation continues to attract many followers.

650–750
Islam spreads by means of traders from the South and invaders from the North and West.

1206–1256
Invasion of the Ottoman Turks. Hinduism coexists with Islam.

1498
Vasco de Gama arrives on Malabar Coast.

1526–1761
Moghul empire: Akbar, descendant of Genghis Khan, creates centralized government and promotes religious tolerance.

1852
British rule established. Campaign to suppress Thuggee cult after crime sprees follow celebration of the goddess Kali.

1920s
Mahatma Gandhi opens first college of Ayurvedic medicine. Sri Aurobindo founds yoga ashram at Pondicherry to promote knowledge of the Self.

1940
Sai Baba declares himself the incarnation of an Indian saint.

1947
Partition of India and Pakistan.

1957
Worldwide revival of yoga.

1967
The Beatles meet the Maharishi Mahesh Yogi, founder of Transcendental meditation, in Rishikesh.

1968
New age settlement, known as Auroville, founded near Pondicherry.

1980s
Growth of Kashmiri and Khalisani nationalism expresses Muslim and Sikh demands for self-determination.

1990s
Ayurvedic revival follows the publication of Deepak Chopra's best-selling book *Ageless Body, Timeless Mind.*

Hinduism

Hinduism grew over a period of 4,000 years in parallel with the cultural developments of the Indian subcontinent. Its roots lie in the sacred writings of the *Veda*, introduced by the Aryans who invaded northwest India in 1,500 B.C.

Lift up the self by the Self;
Let not the self slump down.
For the Self is the self's only friend,
And the self is the Self's only foe.
Bhagavad Gita

In composing the Veda, the invaders assimilated various native religious ideas: Hinduism today encompasses a whole range of beliefs and schools of thought, including tribal practices such as animism and magic. The first Vedas, including the well known Rig-Veda, were complex prose and verse formulas to be pronounced by the priest performing the sacrifice. Later came the Upanishads, speculative and mystical scriptures that set out to explain the source and controlling power of the world. These focus on the doctrine of *Brahman*, the absolute reality, and the achievement through mystical transcendence of *atman*, the true individual self or soul. Also central is the doctrine of *karma*, according to which we reap the results of our good and bad actions through a succession of lifetimes.

Hinduism has no well defined ecclesiastical system and emphasizes the direct religious experience. Hindus believe that an ultimate unity underlies the multiple facets of the world, personified in the deity of the Brahma. As well as this supreme entity, there are many other spirits, devils, and gods, chief of which are Vishnu, the preserver, and Shiva, the destroyer. Vishnu has been reincarnated many times, most notably as Rama and Krishna.

The teacher or guru is central to Hindu practice, which varies widely in style from ascetic to orgiastic, with emphasis commonly placed on yoga, meditation, chanting, and ritual. Some of these forms have been adopted by other spiritual traditions. Buddhism, in particular, has developed many of them in its own way.

HOUSE OF THE GODS
Temple architecture varies throughout India. This temple from Goa, West India, displays the characteristic white paintwork and architectural carving of the region, with the Hindu wheel symbol decorating the outside wall.

Similar wisdoms: The concept of the Unity of Brahma, together with the dual entities of Vishnu and Shiva, corresponds closely to Chinese Taoism, in which the original Oneness is combined with the balancing forces of Yin and Yang.

BRAHMA AND VISHNU

According to Hindu tradition, Brahma (near right) is the creator of the universe, and Vishnu (far right) is its preserver and supporter. The visualization of the deities was codified by Brahmin priests in the Manasara text of the fifth and sixth centuries A.D.

INNUMERABLE INCARNATIONS

Below: The Hindu Gods are represented in various forms in accordance with descriptive legends of the holy texts.

SHIVA AS GODDESS

Above: In Hindu scriptures, Shiva is represented as both male and female, with corresponding destructive and creative qualities that proceed from the divine essence. This bronze figurine from Chola, South India, portrays Shiva in the female form.

THE STEED OF LORD SHIVA

Left: Nandi, Shiva's horse, is widely honored in Hindu art and sculpture. During religious festivities, deities are dressed with garlands of flowers and paper decorations.

Shiva the Destroyer

Vishnu as a bear

Vishnu as a dwarf

Vishnu as Rama

Vishnu as a fish

Concepts of Hinduism

The concept of reincarnation was first documented in the Sanskrit poem Bhagavad-Gita, one of the classic Hindu texts. It suggests that the human soul continues to exist after death, and must pass through countless other births, lives, and deaths in other life forms. Hinduism sees this as an unfortunate process, perpetuated by man's attachment to the material world.

STRUGGLING FOR PERFECTION
The way to spiritual transcendence is through self-mastery, self-denial, and intense contemplation.

Release from the cycle of reincarnation is possible only when the individual reaches a complete state of oneness with Brahma. This is an example of the ancient Eastern view that time is essentially circular or cyclical, rather than linear, as it is seen to be in the West.

There is great interest in the concept of past lives and reincarnation within New Age philosophy. Many therapists now specialize in this field, using methods such as regression and hypnosis. However, some schools of New Age thought assert that the concept of past lives is only a metaphor for explaining our connection with past or future events. Other possible explanations include the idea that time is cyclical, or that there may be a form of shared or collective consciousness.

Karma

The principle of karma is the universal law of cause and effect. It recognizes that as well as their more obvious outward impact, all thoughts and actions have a subtle effect on their perpetrator's life. These karmic effects will be appropriate and relevant to the original action. This is recognized in many other faiths; for example in Christianity, with its frequently quoted teaching, "As ye sow, so shall ye reap." Just as harmful actions create negative effects, compassionate or beneficial thoughts or actions create positive ones. Some karmic effects manifest themselves immediately, while others may not appear for some time. Karma can carry through from one lifetime to another, and families, societies, or even countries are affected by karmic patterns.

The principle of karma is increasingly attractive to Westerners in the New Age. However, the emphasis is shifting from a deterministic explanation of misfortune or disaster, to the view that individuals can create positive karma for themselves and others in the future.

Similar wisdoms: Reincarnation, signifying the continuity and unity of all life, finds expression in many cultural traditions. Early Christianity accepted it, as did cabalistic Judaism and Islamic sufism. In ancient Egypt, the mythical phoenix (right) was said to return every 500 years from Arabia to Heliopolis, the sun city, where it was burned on an altar and rose again from its own ashes.

THE SACRED RIVER
Left: At Varanasi, Hindus plunge into the sacred River Ganges, which flows through the heart of India, to cleanse themselves spiritually and physically.

Tantra

Tantra, the esoteric tradition of ritual and yoga, is a Hindu practice that also exists, although with some significant differences, within Buddhism. A highly specialized form of spiritual philosophy known for its elaborate use of *mantra*, or mystical words, and *mandala*, or sacred diagrams, it employs complex concepts and techniques designed to lead to spiritual enlightenment by very specific paths. These are traditionally only revealed to initiates, and are passed personally from guru to disciple.

In Hindu Tantra, practice is graded into three levels – Animal, Heroic, and finally Divine – through which the initiate may progress with time. Tantric meditation aims at the identification of the devotee's entire being, both mental and physical, with the chosen deity. This is achieved through internal meditation, using a mantra or a mandala as a focus, and outward rituals involving the use of wine, meat, and sexual intercourse. The object of the ritual is the awakening of *kundalini* energy, which is identified with the female deities, or Shakti. Kundalini is the latent power that normally lies coiled at the base of the spine and which, in a devotee of the Divine level, can be made to surge upward through the body's energy centers to the crown of the head, producing a profound flash of enlightenment.

One of the aims of Tantric sexual practice is the unification of the male and female forces of Shiva and Shakti. All around the world the spiritual potential of sexuality has been used to intensify physical reality, thus producing connection with the creative energy of the universe. Tantric sex and sex therapy have become key transformative methods in the New Age.

Gurus

The word guru is formed from the Sanskrit words *gu*, meaning darkness, and *ru*, meaning light. So the guru is one who leads from darkness into light. Gurus first appeared in Hinduism, but they have equivalents in many other forms of spirituality. They are spiritual teachers who help their devotees to achieve enlightenment by example, experience, or direct transmission, rather than by intellectual means. Some gurus are said to be avatars, or actual incarnations of God. Most are extremely charismatic figures.

Eastern gurus began to attract a large Western following during the 1960s and 1970s. Celebrated Indian gurus include Ramana Maharishi, Sri Aurobindo, and Anandamayi Ma. One of the most widely followed worldwide is Sai Baba, reputedly a living avatar. He is alleged to be able to perform miracles, or *siddhis*, and has set up schools, universities, and hospitals offering free treatment. Sai Baba's message is that, through love and selfless service, we can all awaken our soul and discover God within. Some gurus, however, have attracted controversy or scandal, or been exposed as charlatans.

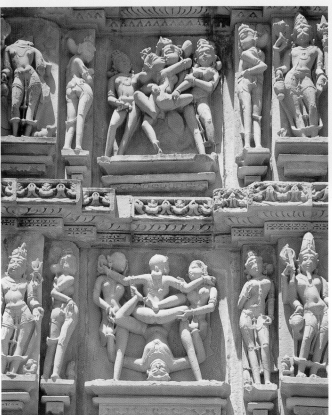

Similar wisdoms: Many other Eastern spiritual traditions have teachers who work in similar ways. There have also been many modern guru figures and inspirational teachers in the West, such as Krishnamurti, Ram Dass, the Russian teacher George Gurdjieff, Rudolf Steiner, and Alice Bailey, to name but a few.

STUDIES IN SUBLIMATION
Left: The wall carvings at Khajurho in the Indian state of Madya Pradesh show sex techniques directed toward spiritual enlightenment.

TANTRIC SEX

Left: Indian art glorifies the sexual delights of Tantra, which employs advanced yogic positions in the quest for spiritual perfection.

VESSEL FOR LIFE

Right: This eighteenth-century Gujerati image shows an image of Cosmic Man holding the Tantric principles of physical movement as a path to spiritual enlightenment.

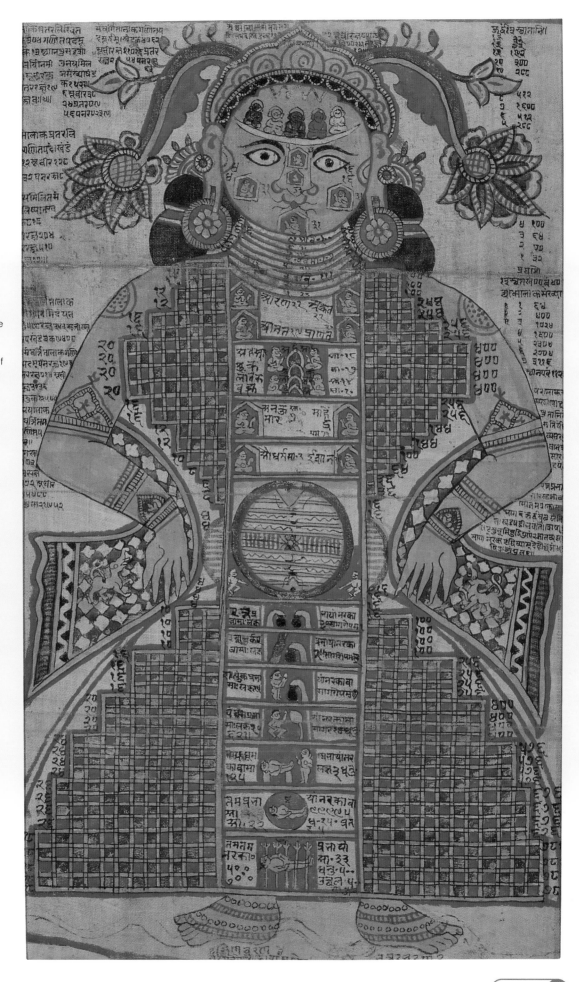

Yoga

The word yoga comes from the same root as the English word yoke, implying a link or union with the divine. A general term for spiritual disciplines in both Hindu and Buddhist traditions whose aim is the attainment of higher consciousness, yoga has many branches: bhakti yoga, the discipline of devotion, mantra yoga, involving repeated chanting, and karma yoga, which sees work as a spiritual practice, are some of the better known.

OM MANTRA
Om may be the earliest evocation of the divine.

In Western New Age awareness, however, the physical forms of yoga have had the most impact. Yogis began to visit the West around the end of the nineteenth century, but it was in the 1960s that yoga underwent a huge explosion in popularity. This was partly because of the burgeoning interest in Eastern spirituality, but also due to the extraordinary benefits that yoga can bring in dealing with the stress of modern life.

Within the yoga of physical postures, or *asana*, there are now a number of especially popular schools in the West. Hatha yoga is one of these. It is concerned with the development and control of the physical body through breathing, so that it does not impede the mind's quest for enlightenment.

Particular yoga teachers, such as Iyengar, have evolved their own individual style. Using these methods, millions of yoga enthusiasts have discovered an improvement in health, strength, and suppleness, peace of mind, and a heightened state of consciousness. Many go on to explore aspects of spirituality arising from other disciplines, such as meditation.

Mantras

A mantra is a word or phrase that influences the mind through its continuous repetition, or through constant focus upon it. It can be uttered silently or aloud, and plays a key part in many yogic practices such as meditation. Individual mantras have specific powers or meaning. In practices such as transcendental meditation, gurus often give a unique mantra to individual followers. Other mantras are chosen or created by the practitioners themselves, and may be used for life. The power of the mantra grows the more it is used. The oldest mantra, and probably the earliest evocation of the divine, is the Hindu word Om.

> **Similar wisdoms:** Many other spirtual traditions use mantras. In Buddhism, the phrase Nam-Myoho-Renge-Kyo, chanted aloud, enables the seeker to find the Buddha within. Tibetans chant Aum-Mani-Padme-Hum, meaning "Hail to the jewel inside the lotus."

LINK WITH THE DIVINE
The Salute to the Sun is one of the most famous yoga sequences. It is traditionally performed in the morning, facing East, and strengthens all parts of the body. The individual yoga postures are called asanas.

Stand upright with hands in the Namaste position

Reach up and lean back

Bend forward and touch the ground

Bring the left leg forward between the hands, looking up

Lower the body to the floor

Similar wisdoms: In New Age culture, many new physical regimes have evolved to help people deal with the effects of modern living. The Alexander technique, for instance, reeducates the body in order to correct habits of bad posture. Similarly, the Feldenkrais method involves relearning patterns of movement to improve quality of life.

THE SUN GOD

Detail from the thirteenth-century A.D. Hindu temple of the sun god Surya at Konorak, eastern India, commissioned by a maharaja to counter the influence of Islam.

Support the body in a straight line

Lower the body to the floor

Bring the right leg forward between the hands, looking up

Bend forward and touch the ground

Reach up and lean back

Stand straight to finish

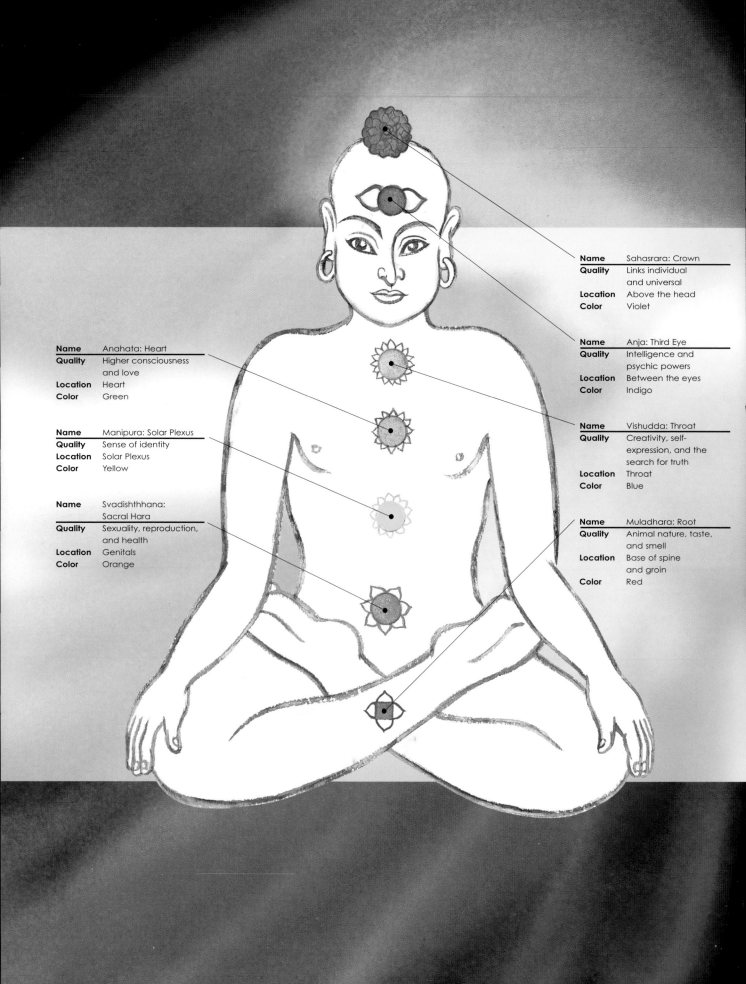

Name   Anahata: Heart
Quality   Higher consciousness
           and love
Location   Heart
Color   Green

Name   Manipura: Solar Plexus
Quality   Sense of identity
Location   Solar Plexus
Color   Yellow

Name   Svadishthhana:
           Sacral Hara
Quality   Sexuality, reproduction,
           and health
Location   Genitals
Color   Orange

Name   Sahasrara: Crown
Quality   Links individual
           and universal
Location   Above the head
Color   Violet

Name   Anja: Third Eye
Quality   Intelligence and
           psychic powers
Location   Between the eyes
Color   Indigo

Name   Vishudda: Throat
Quality   Creativity, self-
           expression, and the
           search for truth
Location   Throat
Color   Blue

Name   Muladhara: Root
Quality   Animal nature, taste,
           and smell
Location   Base of spine
           and groin
Color   Red

The human energy field

The ancient wisdom of the Indian subcontinent is at the root of New Age awareness of the body's subtle energies, and how they can be harnessed. The two main forms of this energy are the auras and the chakras.

The word chakra means wheel of light in Sanskrit. The chakras are the body's internal energy centers. Energy enters the human field from the heavens above and from the earth beneath, meeting within the body. The chakras are therefore a series of seven vortex points or power centers where these forces mingle, each producing a distinctive energy pattern. They are aligned vertically through the center of the body, near the spine. Their function is to absorb, transform and distribute the body's internal energies, the life force or *prana*.

The chakras are interconnected with physical health, including the functions of the organs and glands, and with the emotions, spiritual development, and aspects of personality. In a healthy individual, all the chakras are properly balanced and there is a natural flow of energy through them. However, if some are too weak or too strong, or if there is a blockage in the flow, there will be a corresponding distortion or disharmony in patterns of health. The condition and balance of the chakras can be enhanced through methods such as meditation or visualization. Particular vocalized sounds are also used to vibrate with the corresponding chakras.

Auras

The aura is an electromagnetic field that surrounds the human form, marking an outer boundary between the body and its surroundings. Animals, plants, and even rocks also possess auras.

Similar wisdoms: The notion of a visible, colored emanation surrounding the head or body of an enlightened individual is common to many religious and spiritual traditions. It is a recurrent theme of religious art, from Buddhist, through early Greek and Roman, to Christian depictions, where it is known variously as a nimbus, aureole, or halo.

Colors and changes in an individual's aura can be used to diagnose physical health and spiritual well-being. The quality of the aura's energy also has a powerful influence on other people. Clear and bright coloring indicates a healthy condition that can influence others positively. Dark or muddy colors show an unhealthy or negative disposition that can make others feel tired or depressed. Individual colors in the aura each have a particular meaning. Many people have trained themselves to see these colors and effects, but almost everyone senses them unconsciously.

Auras of particular colors are traditionally associated with different stages in a person's spiritual development. These have been consistently represented by many different cultures; for instance, spiritually advanced beings have often been depicted in paintings with auras of yellow or gold around the head.

The body's aura can now be photographed using Kirlian photography. This is a method developed by a Russian electrical technician, and it is widely used in New Age circles.

RECORDING THE AURAS

Above and right: Kirlian photography displays changes in human energy fields after healing. The image above shows gaps in the second, third, and fifth chakras, while the image to the right shows a more even field.

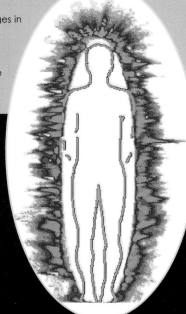

Buddhism

As much a philosophy as a religion, Buddhism offers a radical and practical path to individual peace and purposefulness. This may be why it has had such phenomenal success in the West in the New Age.

The wheel is a key symbol in Buddhism, and represents the concept of reincarnation.

Buddha means "the enlightened one," or "he who knows." The historical figure known as Sakyamuni Buddha was born Siddhartha Gautama, the son of a king of the Sakya clan, in the Himalyan foothills of south Nepal, and lived from 563 B.C. to 483 B.C. Siddhartha spent his youth in luxury, married, and fathered a son. At the age of twenty-nine he abandoned the life of hedonism to seek enlightenment through wandering asceticism in India. Through long meditation he realized that both extremes of austerity and indulgence were futile, and that spiritual realization lay along the Middle Way. Until his death at the age of eighty, he spent his life traveling and teaching the principles of enlightenment, and establishing a community of monks, known as the sangha, to carry on his work. Later, his disciples wrote down these teachings in scriptures known as the Sutras.

As a product of its time, Buddhism accepted the prevailing Indian doctrine of *samsara*, or bondage in repeated cycles of death and rebirth, and Sakyamuni Buddha is recognized as only one of a continuing line of Buddhas who have been incarnated over long periods of history. In contrast to the Vedic tradition, however, Buddhism rejected the caste system, in what was then a radical departure.

Buddhism offers its adherents an end to personal suffering, which they believe arises from attachment to the transient and impermanent. Using the contemplative disciplines of meditation and chanting, it brings freedom from personal delusion, and deeper understanding of the nature of self. Compassion for all living beings is also a key feature.

UNIVERSAL ROLE MODEL OF ENLIGHTENMENT

A depiction of Buddha in a monastery in Ladakh in the Indus Valley, near Nepal, where he was born in the sixth century B.C.

VISUAL AIDS

Highly intricate symbolic diagrams, or mandalas, are used to facilitate contemplation. This one is from a Tibetan monastery, and displays the stylistic elements specific to Tibetan art.

Originating in northern India, Buddhism now has 250 million adherents throughout the world. Most are still in Asia and Japan, but its beliefs and practices appeal to growing numbers of people in Western industrialized countries.

SIXTH CENTURY B.C.

INDIA

c. 563 B.C. Birth of Siddharta Gautama, Sakyamuni Buddha. Early teachings spread through an oral tradition

HINAYANA BUDDHISM

Hinayana (lesser vehicle) Buddhism crystalizes in first century B.C.

MAHAYANA BUDDHISM

Mahayana (greater vehicle) Buddhism crystalizes in first century B.C.

FIRST CENTURY B.C.

FIFTH-SECOND CENTURY B.C.

THIRD CENTURY B.C.

Buddhism enters Sri Lanka

INDIA

Invasions of Huns in sixth century and Muslims in eleventh century almost wipes Buddhism out

FIRST-FIFTH CENTURY A.D.

SPREAD TO CHINA AND KOREA

Scripts translated

SEVENTH CENTURY A.D.

TWENTIETH CENTURY A.D.

FIRST CENTURY B.C.

SIXTH CENTURY A.D.

INTO TIBET

VAJRAYANA Tantric Buddhism

INTO JAPAN

First Buddhist images and texts received from Korea

TIBET

Refugees flee to India after Chinese communist takeover

SRI LANKA

Pali scriptures are finalized, codifying the Buddhist canon for southern Asia

FIRST-FIFTH CENTURY A.D.

SOUTH EAST ASIA

Burma, Thailand

The Spread of Buddhism

Today there are over 250 million Buddhists throughout the world. They follow a belief system that has an unrivaled capacity for being adapted by different cultures, as it merges naturally with the spiritual traditions already existing there. Ironically, Buddhism has flourished more vigorously abroad than in its native India, although it has had a profound effect on Hinduism.

In the third century B.C., the Indian emperor Asoka greatly strengthened Buddhism by his support, sending missionaries north and west as far afield as Syria. The other direction of expansion was southward: Sri Lanka received early scriptures in the third century B.C. and Buddhism remains the national religion today. Buddhism entered China along trade routes from central Asia in the first century A.D., and over the next four centuries spread throughout southeast Asia. It was brought to Tibet in the seventh century, where it flourished. From China and Korea, Buddhism was imported into Japan.

Soon after the Buddha's death, a number of different sects arose, but our knowledge of these is limited as the earliest written texts date from the first century A.D. By this time, there were two broad branches – Hinayana, meaning the lesser vehicle, which includes the Therevada school, and Mahayana, meaning the greater vehicle. A third branch, Vajrayana, is confined largely to Tibet.

Hinayana Buddhism is the predominant form in countries such as Thailand, Sri Lanka and Burma. It emphasizes the meditative and ascetic monastic life as the means whereby the cycle of samsara, or birth and rebirth, is broken, and entry to nirvana is achieved. In these countries, society supports the mendicant monks in order to gain spiritual merit.

OUTPOSTS IN ASIA

Right: Buddhism's influence in the world's most populous continent is illustrated in India and China (top left and right), and Nepal and Burma (bottom left and right).

Mahayana Buddhism and its variants is practiced in north and east Asia, China, Mongolia, Korea, and Japan. It is less austere in its practices, and encourages individuals to seek not only personal enlightenment, but to take compassionate action to help others do the same. Mahayana has developed distinctive forms in all these different locations. In Japan, there are a number of different styles, of which Nichiren is one of the better known. It was founded in the thirteenth century and has now spread to over a hundred other countries.

The twelfth century Mongol empire included all of China and large portions of central Asia. These people converted wholesale to Buddhism by edict of the emperor Kublai Khan.

Tibetan Buddhism is an extremely colorful and ritualistic form that retains much of the shamanism and sorcery of Bon, an ancient animistic religion of Tibet. It is derived from Vajrayana, a subset of Mahayana, but much of its ritual is based on the esoteric mysticism of Tantra. Tantric Buddhism

asserts that the individual already has enlightenment within, and can discover it through private guidance by a spiritual master. The leading monastic lamas, known as Tulkus, are seen as reincarnating repeatedly into the same monastic role. Each time a Tulku dies, the process of scouring Tibet begins to find his reincarnated successor. In the last century, these reincarnations have begun to occur among non-Tibetans in other parts of the world. The Dalai Lama is one of the most significant figures in this tradition, and has had considerable personal influence on many world leaders. China invaded Tibet in the 1950s, suppressing this religion and destroying many monasteries.

Many of these styles of Buddhism have spread from their country of development to the West, and Buddhism is now the world's fastest growing religion, partly because of the absence of both a personalized god figure and concepts such as original sin or a burden of guilt.

Meditation

Meditation is a long-proven approach to self-knowledge, self-awareness, and self-realization, often experienced in the form of conventional prayer. Buddhism has developed it into its highest forms, and has inspired its introduction to the modern world.

The fundamental aim of meditating is, by focusing or concentrating the mind, to let go of distractions and to exist fully in the present moment. It is particularly attractive as an antidote to modern materialism and spiritual emptiness. It is also accessible, and can be experienced without adherence to religion, as millions of individuals from all walks of life are now finding.

The regular practice of meditation brings a wide range of benefits through its influence on the mind. It reduces brain activity and creates a sense of relaxation and calm, it regulates blood pressure and reduces emotional stress. Many prominent celebrities have espoused its practice. The singer Tina Turner, for instance, reports that meditation has changed her whole life. Meditation can take many forms: it can consist simply of focusing on the breath, or on thoughts as they come and go; or it can be extremely advanced and esoteric. Specialized forms of meditation include Meta Bhavana, or the practice of loving kindness, meditation on sound or a visual image, movement meditation, and chanting with a mantra.

Traditional yogic wisdom recognizes that, over time and with practice, meditation naturally releases *siddhis* – psychic and magical powers, such as telepathy, levitation or the ability to recall past lives. These faculties are not regarded as significant in themselves, but many New Age practitioners of meditation find that some of them develop spontaneously after a number of years.

FLOWER POWER

Concentrating the mind on a restful image, such as a flower, is among a number of special techniques for meditation.

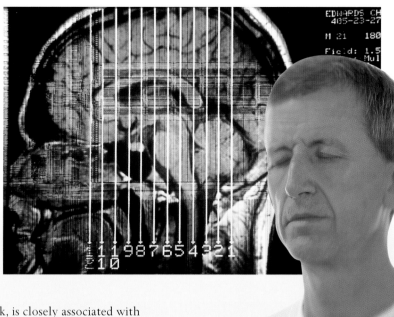

THE RIGHT WAVELENGTH

Modern medical equipment can measure and record the physical effects of systematic meditation, such as lowering brainwave activity and blood pressure. These effects improve the overall condition of the body, and help reduce the risk of strokes and heart failure.

Visualization

Visualization, or image work, is closely associated with meditation. It involves the conscious process of creating images in the mind for spiritual or transformative purposes. It is an ancient procedure that plays an important part in almost all spiritual and magical traditions. Elaborate visualization is central, for instance, to Tibetan Buddhism. For New Age practitioners, it is an activity in its own right. Sometimes referred to as creative visualization or manifestation, it has brought increased success, fulfilment, and happiness to many thousands of people.

Similar wisdoms: A number of New Age methods use techniques similar to those of meditation and visualization to harness the power of thought. Autogenic training uses visualization for specific goals such as getting to sleep or improving performance in sports. Sylva Mind Control and Positive Thinking both seek to use the power of thought to improve life experience. Neuro-Linguistic Programming or NLP works by identifying patterns of thought that lead to effective communication, accelerated learning, positive change, and greater enjoyment of life.

CHINA AND JAPAN

Ever since Marco Polo brought back wondrous tales of the East, the rich spiritual heritage of China and Japan has fascinated the West. Over the centuries, and especially in the last 100 years, many facets of Oriental culture – from martial arts, through acupuncture, to Chinese medicine – have been enthusiastically adopted, to the extent that they now seem almost mainstream. Others, such as taoism, shiatsu, and zazen meditation, have long had adherents in the West. Most recently the New Age Movement has introduced ancient systems like Feng Shui and the I Ching to a new generation.

TIME LINE

5000 B.C.
Neolithic communities farm, fish, and raise animals. Silk and pottery also produced.

2852 B.C.
Fu Hsi is said to have created the trigrams.

c. 1994–1523 B.C.
Writing is invented.

1750–1040 B.C.
Bones gain popularity as divination tool.

1231–1135 B.C.
Wen Wang writes the I Ching.

722–221 B.C.
With the defeat of the Zhou dynasty, China enters a period of great violence and change.

604–531 B.C.
Lao Tzu, credited as the founder of Taoism, writes the Tao Te Ching.

551–479 B.C.
Kong Zi (Confucius) encourages a return to tradition. The *Analects of Confucius*, a compilation of his teachings, is published after his death.

221–207 B.C.
Unification of China. China's first emperor and his terracotta army are entombed, not to be discovered until 1974.

106 B.C.
Cai Lun invents paper.

c.100 B.C.
Buddhism introduced into China by way of India and Central Asia, but not established until the Tang dynasty (618–906 A.D.).

206 B.C.–220 A.D.
Confucianism at center of system of government.

398
Datong is chosen as capital of Northern Wei dynasty. Work begins on monumental Buddhist statues in Yungang caves.

581–618
Extension of Great Wall.

618–906
Islam reaches China. Golden age of arts. Lama Buddhism develops in Tibet at the expense of

KEY

This key indicates the main areas of anthropological and religious significance.

 Buddhist rock carvings and cave paintings

 Lamaist Buddhist monasteries

 Sacred Mountains

 Great Wall of China

Western provinces convert to Islam during the Tang dynasty (618–706 A.D.). These regions are still mainly Muslim despite the influx of Han Chinese and the banning of religion during the Cultural Revolution.

Kublai Khan (1215–1294) reunified China and helped spread Lamaist Buddhism. The cultural exchanges which followed resulted in the building of Mongolian monasteries as far south as Tibet, at Sakya for example, and Tibetan monasteries being built in Mongolia. During the Mongol period (1271–1368) Chinese astrology and animal imagery became widespread. Right: In Tibet, Lamaist Buddhist scriptures were painted onto large stones and kept as prayer aids.

The Silk Road carried not only goods from east to west, but also art, ideas, and religion. Judaism also found its way east along the Silk Road. A pocket long persisted in Kaifeng.

Mount Kailash is holy to the indigenous religion of Tibet, Bon. It is also sacred to Hindus as the birthplace of Shiva.

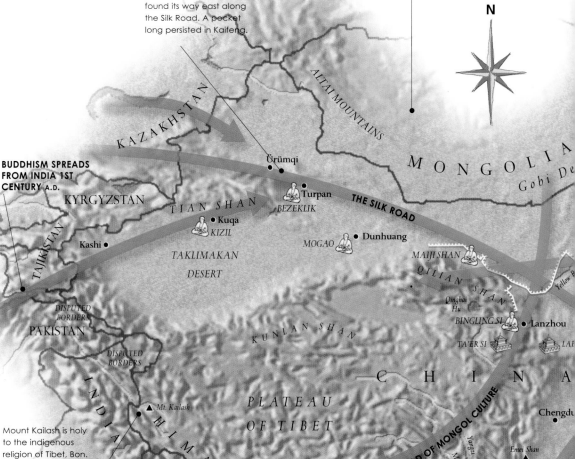

BUDDHISM SPREADS FROM INDIA 1ST CENTURY A.D.

TIBETAN COMMUNITY FLEE TO INDIA AFTER 1950

THE SILK ROAD

SPREAD OF MONGOL CULTURE

KAZAKHSTAN

KYRGYZSTAN

TAJIKISTAN

PAKISTAN

DISPUTED BORDERS

DISPUTED BORDERS

INDIA

NEPAL

BHUTAN

HIMALAYAS

▲ Mt. Kailash

▲ Mt. Everest

PLATEAU OF TIBET

KUNLAN SHAN

TAKLIMAKAN DESERT

TIAN SHAN

Kashi ●

Kuqa
KIZIL

Ürümqi

Turpan
BEZEKLIK

MOGAO

● Dunhuang

MAIJI SHAN

QILIAN SHAN

Qinghai Hu

TA'ER SI

BINGLING SI

● Lanzhou

LA...

C H I N A

Chengdu

Emei Shan

Yangzi

Mekong

Salween

● Lhasa

SAKYA

Brahmaputra

ALTAI MOUNTAINS

M O N G O L I A

Gobi De...

Yellow R.

● Kunmi...

BURMA

LAOS

VIET...

N

China

Map labels

NOMADS, SUCH AS THE
OROQEN, INVADE
FROM SIBERIA

R U S S I A

Amur

Manchurian
Plain

• Qiqihar

• Harbin

Jilin •

Changchun •

• Chongjin

Fushun •

NORTH
KOREA

*Sea of
Japan*

Shenyang •
Anshan •

• Sinuiju

DA HINGGAN LING

ner Mongolia

Inner Mongolia

■ PYONGYANG
• Nampo

Dalian •

ong

BEIJING ■
PYUNGANG
▲ Wutai Shan
Tianjin •

Tangshan •

Inchon • ■ SEOUL

SOUTH • Taegu
KOREA • Pusan

• Taiyuan
• Shijiazhuang

Jinan • • Zibo

• Qingdao

AD OF KONG ZI'S
OPHY (CONFUCIANISM)
CROSS CHINA

▲ Tai Shan

• Qufu

*Yellow
Sea*

CH'AN BUDDHISM
EXPORTED TO JAPAN,
WHERE IT BECOMES
KNOWN AS ZEN

SHAOLIN
NGMEN • Kaiting

• Luoyang

'an

TAOISM
SPREADS
TO TAIWAN

Yellow River

P A C I F I C

Huainan •

▲ Wudang Shan

Nanjing •

Shanghai •

Emei Shan ▲

• Ningbo

Wuhan •

Yangtze

Hangzhou •

O C E A N

*Donting
Hu*

Nanchang •

*Poyang
Hu*

Wenzhou •

*East
China
Sea*

Changsha •

Fuzhou •

■ TAIPEI

Zhangzhou •

TAIWAN

Guilin •

Guangzhou • • Kowloon
Macao • • Hong Kong

The first Feng Shui manual
based on the features of the
landscape was produced
around 840–880 A.D. In it,
Feng Shui master Yang Yun
Sung described the
spectacular limestone
scenery at Guilin (right).

*South
China
Sea*

HAINAN

Spirituality in China

Ancient Chinese belief systems included
animistic religions and ancestor worship.
Oracular practices were formalized into
all-encompassing divination methods,
such as the I Ching.

By the fifth century B.C., two major
philosophies had evolved. Confucianism
was a system of ethics based on the
teachings of Kong Zi (Confucius), and it
continues to influence Chinese thought
today. Taoism, associated with the sage
Lao Tzu, focused on the energies of the
natural world, and is at the root of
many Chinese disciplines such as Tai
Chi. Buddhism was imported from
India around 200 B.C., and is the third
main influence on Chinese spirituality.
It developed various forms in Southeast
Asia, including Zen in Japan, and is
treated in more detail in the chapters
on India and Japan. Legend has it that
Kong Zi, Lao Tzu, and the Buddha were
alive at the same time, but no one
knows whether these figures really
existed or whether their works
represent a collective achievement.

These three spiritual influences
mingle in Chinese culture, to the
extent that it is often difficult to
identify the separate schools of
thought. That all three, together with
China's ancient folk religions, survived
through the myriad political, social,
and religious changes of the twentieth
century is a testament to how much an
integrated part of the culture they are.

the indigenous Bon
shamanistic religion.

1126–1271
Invention of moveable
type.

1271–1368
Genghis Khan and the
Mongols invade. Huge
Mongolian monastery
built at Sakya in Tibet;
Lamaist Buddhism
favored by Kublai Khan.

1368–1644
Hong Wu, a former monk,
takes control from the
Mongols and establishes
himself as first emperor of
the Ming dynasty. End of
trade and contact with
outside world.

1644–1911
The Potala Palace in
Lhasa, Tibet, is rebuilt by
the fifth Dalai Lama. Inner
Mongolia, Outer
Mongolia, Tibet, and
Turkestan come under
Manchu control.

1912
Republican government
takes over; Confucianism
no longer used as system
of government.

1945
Civil war between
Kuomintang and People's
Liberation Army.

1949
Communist government
under Mao Zedong;
country becomes
increasingly closed to
Western influence.

1950
China invades Tibet.

1958
Chinese land organized
into communes.

1959
Dalai Lama escapes to
India. Temples and
monasteries destroyed in
the ensuing suppression.

1966–1968
Destruction of
ideologically unsound art
in Cultural Revolution.

1980s
Open Door Policy follows
Nixon's visit in 1972. Many
temples, monasteries, and
mosques are reopened in
China and Tibet.

1989
Democratic movement
suppressed in Tiananmen
Square incident.

1997
Hong Kong handed back
to China by Great Britain.

Chinese cosmology

The ancient concepts of yin and yang, ch'i (or life energy), and the five elements form the basis of many traditional Chinese disciplines such as acupuncture, qigong, traditional Chinese medicine, and tai ch'i, all of which have been rediscovered by the New Age Movement.

In the ancient Chinese model for understanding the cosmos, there is an undifferentiated source, or whole, from which everything else is differentiated in an infinite, progressive process. This original source is the Tao, or Dao.

The fundamental concepts of classical Chinese philosophy were laid down during the Chou dynasty (c. 1027–256 B.C.). The writings of Kong Zi (Confucius), Lao Tzu, and Chuang-Tsu were collated and expanded by later scholars to form a formalized code of Confucianism and Taoism, with guides on divination, government, the arts, and education.

NOTE ON THE SPELLING
It is now usual practice to transliterate Chinese characters into Pinyin, but throughout this chapter and elsewhere, the older, more familiar spellings have been retained where they are widely recognized. Hence we use *ch'i*, but prefer the modern form in the compound *qigong* (rather than *ch'i kung*). Similarly the familiar *tao te ching* is retained in preference to the Pinyin *dao de jing*.

The Tao gave birth to the One
The One gave birth to the Two
The Two gave birth to the Three
The Three gave birth to the Ten Thousand Things

Lao Tzu * *Tao Te Ching*

THE TAO OF WISDOM
In Lao Tzu's descriptive verse, above, the Tao refers to the originating source; the Two are the polarizing tendencies of yin and yang, and the Three are water, earth, and heaven. The Ten Thousand Things are the myriad other things that also exist in the world.

Cosmic Forces

In contrast to the Judeo-
Christian concept of a
Supreme Being as creator,
the traditional Chinese view
holds that the universe was
created by impersonal cosmic forces.
Humans have an important role to play
in its continuing development, as mankind is
responsible for maintaining balance in the universe. This is the
reason why promoting a healthy balance of ch'i forms the basis
of many Chinese disciplines. Feng Shui, for example, aims to
improve the flow of ch'i through a given environment, and
the breathing exercises of qigong are designed to balance ch'i
within the body.

In the Chinese tradition, spiritual masters use simple stories
to explain complex concepts to their followers, and this folk
tale nicely illustrates the duality of yin and yang:

One day, the master gave his young pupil a coin and asked
him how many sides it had.

"Two," the pupil replied without hesitation. The master
shook his head solemnly, then asked the boy to go away and
ponder the problem. After several days spent deep in thought,
the student returned dejected.

The master put him out of his misery. "The coin has three
sides," he said. "The front, the back, and the ch'i holding them
together. This too is an essential side of the coin."

LAO TZU

At the heart of
classical Chinese
thought are the
teachings of the
Buddha, Confucius,
and Lao Tzu. Their ideas
have become so
intermingled that the
phrase "three teachings
flow into one" is often used
to describe the Chinese
blend of philosophies.

The two qualities yin and
yang are held together by
the essential energy, ch'i.
Below, Lao Tzu explains
that the universe is either
yin (dark) or yang (light),
and that ch'i (the
immaterial breath) holds
the two elements in
balance.

All things are backed by shade
Faced by the light
The Two gave birth to the Three
And harmonized by the immaterial breath

Lao Tzu ★ *Tao Te Ching*

The eight trigrams are a set of symbols developed by Fu Hsi, the first emperor of China. Each one is made up of three broken or solid lines, reflecting yin (negative) and yang (positive) forces. The system records all the different permutations of yin and yang, starting at heaven and earth, and working through all the combinations.

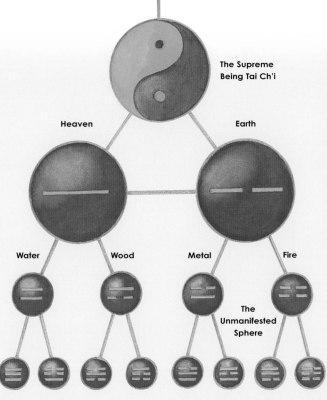

The Unnameable Subtle Origin

The Supreme Being Tai Ch'i

Heaven

Earth

Water   Wood   Metal   Fire

The Unmanifested Sphere

The Manifested Sphere

Applications of Yin and Yang

The origin of yin and yang is traditionally associated with the ancient sage Fu Hsi. In the Chinese view, all life on earth is profoundly affected by these two influences. Yang is the heavenly force, exemplified by the life-giving radiation that showers down from the sun, stars, constellations, and galaxies. It is most obviously embodied in the force of gravity. The other is the opposing, balancing yin force that originates in the center of the earth and expands outward. It is demonstrated by the ability of trees and plants to grow upward.

These two powerful energy fields are found in everything. Yin is associated with all that is dark, female, or cool, while yang is associated with masculinity, light, and heat. However, nothing is purely yin or purely yang. Their combination in any form is always in a constant and dynamic state of opposition and balance. There is a subtle interplay between them, which changes from year to year, season to season, and moment to moment. Monitoring this balance is a vital part of Chinese philosophy, and can be achieved through traditional divination, physical disciplines, and medicine.

THE YIN AND YANG SYMBOL

The circular yin and yang diagram, above, symbolizes the negative and positive principles of life, which are in a constant state of flux. The light half (yang) contains the seed of the dark half (yin). This symbol has been widely adopted by the New Age Movement to represent universal harmony.

Similar wisdoms: The pyramid structure of the trigram permutations mimics the arrangement of the sefirot (spheres) on the Tree of Life from the Jewish Cabala. The transcendent tai ch'i, from which the combinations descend, may be compared to the highest sefira, Keter, The Crown, below which lie the lower earthly sefirot.

ETERNAL CYCLE
The Five Elements are fully
interrelated, and sympathetically
feed into, and interact with,
each other.

Fire

Earth

Wood

Metal

Water

The Five Elements

According to Taoist belief, yin and yang work
together to create the Five Elements: Water, Wood,
Fire, Earth, and Metal. Everything in the universe is
made up of these elements and their physical traits.

This system is more accurately referred to as the Five
Stages of Change. The interplay between yin and yang takes
place in all physical states – expansion and contraction, heat
and cold, and light and dark. There are also intermediate
points within these cycles, between day and night or birth
and death, for example. The Five Elements are regarded as
metaphysical forces rather than real substances, and their
applied meaning is used in Chinese medicine, art, and
philosophy.

The Ten Stems and Twelve Branches

Other forms of classification in Chinese philosophy include
the Ten Celestial Stems and the Twelve Branches. The Stems
are the energies of heaven, and the Branches are the energies
of earth. Both concepts are used within Chinese divination.

PHYSICAL CORRELATIONS OF THE FIVE ELEMENTS

ELEMENT	SEASON	DIRECTION	TASTE	IN SYMPATHY WITH	CONFLICTS WITH
Fire	summer	south	bitter	earth, as fire turns wood to ash, which goes back into the earth	metal, by burning it
Wood	spring	east	sour	fire, as wood supplies the material for the flames	earth, because tree roots break it up
Metal	autumn	west	pungent	water, because metal containers traditionally carry water	wood, because metal axes can chop down trees
Earth	summer	center	sweet	metal, because the earth creates metal within its depths	water, because it turns it to mud
Water	winter	north	salty	wood, because water feeds the trees	fire, because it puts it out

The I Ching

The I Ching is the classical Chinese method of divination. It started as an oral tradition, and was formalized by the great sage Kong Zi (Confucius). The system has been used in Chinese culture since ancient times, and has now entered common usage in the West. It is an all-encompassing system, offering advice on emotional and material aspects of everyday life.

The I Ching indicates a situation's potential by reflecting the interaction of yin and yang at that particular time and place. This interaction is portrayed through symbols known as trigrams and hexagrams.

SACRED TORTOISE
For the Chinese, the tortoise (above) symbolizes longevity, strength, and endurance. Its distinctive shell markings were said to correspond to star constellations, and inspired the mythical emperor Fu Hsi to create the eight trigrams.

The Trigrams and Hexagrams

The use of trigrams and hexagrams originates in Neolithic bone and tortoiseshell divination. The tortoiseshell was heated in a fire, causing a pattern of cracks to appear, which were then interpreted by the diviner. Over a period of time, the patterns were formally inscribed on the shell, which would then be used as a permanent oracle for consultation.

The written characters of the Chinese language evolved from these simple ideograms. Over time, significant patterns of cracks were stylized into eight three-lined diagrams known as trigrams, and the study of these became an art in itself.

The trigrams are made up of combinations of solid (yang) and broken (yin) lines, each signifying a different configuration of yin-yang energies. In due course, definitive meanings came to be assigned to a standardized set of trigrams. From 1100 B.C., these were combined in pairs, making a set of 64 six-lined diagrams called hexagrams. These expressed a much greater range of subtle interactions. Each one had its own commentary, known as a judgment, that outlined its qualities and implications.

As the trigram system developed, it offered clear philosophical guidance for everyday living, as well as divinatory predictions. It became known as the Book of Changes – the I Ching.

Since its formalization, the I Ching has adopted extra commentaries, but remained essentially the same. In the modern era, it has been translated into many other languages. Its popularity exploded in the West in the 1960s, and continues to increase today. In the face of many more superficial forms of oracle, its appeal lies in the depth of its investigation.

CHINESE DIVINATION BONE
The use of oracle bones, such as this Chinese scapula (shoulder blade) was common in the ancient world. However, it was only in China that drilling and heat were used to create cracks. Subjects for divination included military campaigns and the emperor's health, as well as daily matters, such as the weather and prospects for the harvest.

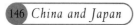

The psychologist Carl Jung did much to open up the West's awareness of the I Ching as a tool for living. His psychological system categorized people on the basis of their behavior, and defined archetypal forms of human development. Both of these elements are reflections of the I Ching system.

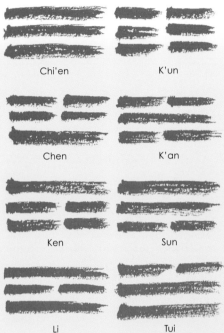

Chi'en   K'un

Chen   K'an

Ken   Sun

Li   Tui

Using Trigrams for Divination

Each trigram has numerous correspondences and attributes, such as natural features, parts of the body, and family relationships. Together they symbolize the evolution of nature and its cyclical changes. The trigrams are a common sight in China where they are believed to bring good luck and prosperity and ward off misfortune. They can also be found on the Korean flag. Any two trigrams can be combined in 64 possible ways to create a hexagram with a complex meaning. These six-lined symbols can be used as a divination tool to show how the world is changing and how the user should react in light of these changes.

I CHING SYMBOLS

The eight trigrams used in the I Ching are each made up of three lines, which can be continuous or broken in two.

ASSOCIATED TRAITS OF THE TRIGRAMS

TRIGRAM	NAME	ASSOCIATED IMAGE	ASSOCIATED ATTRIBUTES	ANIMAL	FAMILY LINK	DIRECTION
ch'ien	heaven	sky	strength, power	horse	father	northwest
k'un	earth	fidelity	submission	ox	mother	southwest
chen	thunder	impulsiveness	provocation	dragon	elder son	east
k'an	water	danger	flexibility	pig	middle son	north
ken	mountain	immobility	inevitability	dog	younger son	northeast
sun	wind	subtlety	penetration	fowl	elder daughter	southeast
li	fire	enlightenment	warmth	pheasant	middle daughter	south
tui	marsh	joy	magic	goat	younger daughter	west

Similar wisdoms: The trigrams and hexagrams of the I Ching have a parallel in the ancient Celtic Ogham system. This also uses combinations of lines to express energies in the natural world, and indicate how they affect human experience.

I CHING COINS

Hexagrams can be constructed with three I Ching coins. Each coin has an unpatterned side, with just two markings on them, and a patterned side, with four Chinese characters around the center.

Unpatterned

Unpatterned

Patterned

Casting the Hexagrams

There are many traditional ways of casting the hexagrams, such as counting yarrow sticks or using rice grains. Nowadays, casting can be done by computer, and a simpler method exists using just three coins – one with a pattern and two without.

Tossing the coins generates one line at a time starting from the bottom, so the coins have to be tossed six times to provide a complete hexagram. If a coin falls with its pattern facing up, the score is two. If it falls with the unpatterned side up, the score is three. Using this system, the only possible scores are six, seven, eight, or nine for each line of the hexagram. The scores for each line are labeled in four ways: yin, yang, moving yin (where the yin is becoming yang,) and moving yang (where the yang is becoming yin.)

Consulting the I Ching

In an average I Ching reading, each line and each hexagram can be interpreted, giving over 11,500 different configurations, covering every possible human situation. It can be consulted to answer a particular question or to understand a specific situation. The individual meditates on his or her question or situation before casting the coins, and should have it in mind throughout to ensure an appropriate response. The coins are then tossed six times to determine each line of the hexagram.

Reading Your Scores

A score of seven is a yang line

A score of eight is a yin line

A score of six is a moving yin

A score of nine is a moving yang

USING YARROW STICKS

Yarrow sticks were traditionally used to cast the hexagrams. Starting with 50 sticks, the diviner counted the sticks into groups, then counted them again to reveal the trigram lines. The traditional illustration below shows the diviner calculating the hexagram scores.

Throw 6 gives 2 patterned and 1 blank
Total score = 7, making a yang line

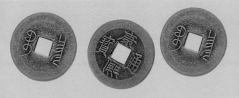

Throw 5 gives 2 blank and 1 patterned
Total score = 8, making a yin line

Throw 4 gives 3 blanks
Total score = 9, making a moving yang line

Throw 3 gives 3 patterned
Total score = 6, making a moving yin line

Throw 2 gives 2 blank and 1 patterned
Total score = 8, making a yin line

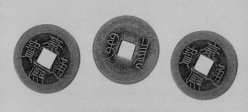

Throw 1 = 2 patterned and 1 blank
Total score is 7, making yang line

Generating a Hexagram

The example below forms the 18th hexagram out of the possible 64. This hexagram is associated with reparation and fixing, and the reading advises the individual to right a wrong that may have occurred.

Throw 6
Throw 5
Throw 4
Throw 3
Throw 2
Throw 1

The moving yin and moving yang lines show that the overall score is shifting towards hexagram 38. This is associated with neutrality, so it is important to consider the original advice in the light of this additional hexagram.

Sample Hexagram Meanings

Below are a selection of readings taken from the 64 possible hexagrams. They are often read in conjunction with the second hexagram towards which the trigrams are moving.

1 YANG
You will achieve your objectives through work and patience. Plan well. Avoid conflict and strain.

3 GROWING PAINS
Learn to advance slowly. Do not set your sights too high. Accept help.

8 SEEKING UNION
Make the most of peaceful times. Cooperate sincerely with others.

17 FOLLOWING
For the moment let others take the lead. Once they have guided you to safety, you may be able to take command.

42 INCREASE
Make the most of good opportunities. Do not expect them to last.

62 SMALLNESS IN EXCESS
Curb your ambitions and be cautious. However weak your position, you will make gains.

Taoism

The Way to Do is to Be — LAO TZU

Along with Confucianism and Buddhism, Taoism is the third great strand of Chinese spirituality. Taoism does not involve the worship of any deity, and is more a life-enhancing philosophy than a religion. It is about finding one's true nature and direction, and the authentic actions to take in keeping with cosmic energies.

The exact meaning of the word Tao is difficult to pin down, but it is often summarized as "The Way." It is the term used in Chinese translations to render the Greek *logos* (word) in the biblical phrase: "In the beginning was the Word." The original Tao was the Ultimate Reality, the first cause of everything that is. It is hard to overstate the influence Taoism has had on all aspects of Chinese thought and culture.

Origins

Lao Tzu, who lived around 2700 years ago, was the founder of formalized Taoism, the principles of which he set out in his classic text, the *Tao Te Ching* – the world's most translated book after the Bible. It is written in abstract, enigmatic verses that allow for great variety of interpretation and humor. Lao Tzu's disciple, Tschuang Tse, expanded his master's work with additional parables and aphorisms.

Similar wisdoms: The tenets of Taoism corresponded closely to the Zen Buddhist concept of positive inaction, which reached its peak in Japan. Cultural exchanges between China and Japan undoubtedly resulted in the two philosophies becoming intertwined on both an abstract and physical level.

The Object of Taoism

The goal of Taoism is the state of Wu-Wei, in which the individual spontaneously stops obstructing the universal flow of the Tao. This is achieved by acting like water, which yields, adapts, and flows around obstacles, yet possesses the power to erode mountains. Acceptance and perseverance, rather than the use of effort and force, are important keys to this.

Historically, Taoism had two branches – esoteric Taoism, the Taoism of sages who either lived as hermits or led a purist life in monasteries, and a simpler popular strand, which was embraced by ordinary people. Esoteric Taoism focused on magical practices, using mastery of interactive energies to generate power. The popular form synthesized many strands of the animistic folk religions of ancient China.

THE TAO OF WATER

Taoism is concerned with the relationship of the individual to nature. In chapter eight of the Tao Te Ching, Lao Tzu asserts that the best of man is like water, because "Water benefits all things and does not oppose them. It is always at rest in humble places that people dislike. Thus it is in harmony with the Tao."

Feng Shui

Feng Shui is the Chinese study of the energy of place. It is used to create harmony and balance within one's living or working environment. The name literally means "wind and water," but it encompasses the whole system of subtle energies in any location. It is based on the concept that to achieve happiness, humanity must integrate properly with nature, and fit into a landscape's patterns of energy rather than dominate them.

This principle applies to the smallest details of an environment, such as its decor and the way its furniture is laid out, because subtle energies can profoundly affect the occupants' peace of mind, health, longevity, and prosperity.

Origins and Development

Originally, Feng Shui was used for the correct siting of graves. Finding auspicious burial sites is an important tradition in Chinese culture, since good luck and prosperity stem from the benevolence of one's ancestors. The Feng Shui master had a monopoly on the essential knowledge, and it was primarily a hereditary profession. Today, yin, or negative, Feng Shui is still used in the search for auspicious burial dates and the correct alignment for graves.

Yang, or positive, Feng Shui is concerned with the effective design of homes and commercial premises in relation to the environment. Today, Feng Shui influences urban planning, architecture, and interior and landscape design. It is used by commercial organizations around the world and there are a number of schools of approach. The Shapes and Form School focuses on the natural landscape and the Five Elements, while the Compass School uses the trigrams and the points of the compass as its principal guide. Each now has various offshoots.

The Feng Shui Consultation

The contemporary Feng Shui master advises on the correct site for building a new house or commercial premises. He determines the appropriate orientation of the building by studying the location with the aid of a *lo pan*, or Chinese compass. He then allocates the various functions to the most appropriate areas of the building: for example, accounting functions and cash registers are traditionally sited in the southeast corner of an office building because of this quadrant's associations with prosperity.

Where a building already exists, the Feng Shui master may suggest "cures" to improve the energy flow. These might include reducing clutter, changing the decor, and positioning mirrors, plants, and crystals to encourage the flow of ch'i.

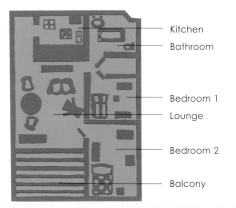

Kitchen
Bathroom

Bedroom 1
Lounge

Bedroom 2

Balcony

BEFORE

Left: The plan shows the positive areas are in the south-eastern bedroom and the west-facing lounge. The north-east and southwest need improvement, and relate to the areas of romance and education.

AFTER

Below: Place mirrors in the northeast corner of the bathroom to extend this part of the room. Put windchimes in the west-facing corridor to move stagnant ch'i.

Good and Bad Ch'i

A major element in Feng Shui is ch'i – the "breath" or current of vital energy that flows through everything. When ch'i is allowed to circulate freely, it brings well-being, good health, and fortune. If ch'i is blocked, trapped, interrupted, or too intensely directed, it has adverse effects. For instance, tall buildings can block the free passage of ch'i, but a river running in front of your house can sweep ch'i in your direction. A straight corridor may propel beneficial ch'i in through one door and out through the other before the benefits are felt.

The Pa Kua

The pa kua is a tool that combines trigrams with numerical and diagnostic information. It is used to assess the energies of a given space and diagnose the effect of the existing arrangement. There are eight versions of the pa kua, each with different environmental information for the patterns of energy that are shown to exist.

The pa kua is used to determine areas of weak and strong Feng Shui in a home, as shown here. It is laid over the floor plan to show which areas correspond to the facets of the occupants' life, health, career, and relationships, for example. Each area is symbolized by a trigram.

RECOGNITION AND FAME
SOUTH
RED
FIRE
LI
SUN
SMALL WOOD
GREEN
SOUTH EAST
WEALTH & PROSPERITY

LOVE & MARRIAGE
SOUTH WEST
YELLOW
STRONG EARTH
K'UN

FAMILY & HEALTH
EAST
GREEN, BROWN
STRONG WOOD
CHEN

CHILDREN
WEST
METALLIC; WHITE; GOLD
SMALL METAL
TUI

KEN
SMALL EARTH
BEIGE
NORTH EAST
EDUCATION & KNOWLEDGE

CH'IEN
STRONG METAL
METALLIC; WHITE; GOLD
NORTH WEST
MENTORS & NETWORKING

K'AN
WATER
BLACK, BLUE
NORTH
CAREER PROSPECTS

AFTER

Put lights and plants in the southwest corner of the balcony to enhance the ch'i, and activate prosperity.

DIRECTING THE FLOW OF CH'I

Left: In Hong Kong, where Feng Shui is widely used in the business environment, mirrors are placed on the southeast side of commercial properties to promote prosperity. They are also placed in corridors to prevent ch'i flowing in a adversely straight line.

The Role of the Five Elements

A key concept for assessing Feng Shui is the principle of the Five Elements. Each element is associated with a shape: Wood is tall and narrow, Fire is triangular, Earth is flat, Metal is circular, and Water is irregular. In the ideal site, no particular shape should dominate the landscape. If this happens, the Feng Shui master will recommend the placing of other objects to balance the effect. For example, placing trees (Wood) around a building with a sharply tapering roof (Fire) would produce a stimulating atmosphere, because the Wood stimulates and is sympathetic to Fire.

The Four Animals

According to ancient Feng Shui practice, certain topographical features promote or modify the flow of ch'i. These are symbolized by the Four Animals that traditionally rule the compass points: the Turtle (North), Dragon (East), Tiger (West), and Phoenix (South).

The Turtle

The Turtle symbolizes the mountain that should back any home or business. Today, it can be substituted by a large building.

The Dragon

Rolling hills, or the Dragon, should be on the east of the house. In modern terms, other houses will fill this role.

The Tiger

Low hills, known as the Tiger, should protect the right side of the house. Houses or garages are acceptable alternatives for the Tiger in an urban environment.

The Phoenix

A gentle stream carrying ch'i along in its flow forms the ideal frontage for a home or office. Roads with moving traffic or a circular driveway are suitable alternatives. The flow is important—if it is stagnant, ch'i deteriorates. If it is too fast, the ch'i disperses.

Left and below left: When the Bank of China was designed and built without consulting a Feng Shui master, surrounding residents rushed to alter the structure of their homes and businesses to correct the ch'i imbalance caused by the 70-floor building. One of their major criticisms was that the bank's extreme angles were said to create arrows of harmful *sha* energy that pierced the surrounding buildings.

Feng Shui at Work

Feng Shui is used to direct positive ch'i through the office and to increase wealth and prosperity. The arrangement of the office must be carefully thought out once the diagnosis is made – for example, partitions should be avoided where they block the natural flow of ch'i.

The position of the desk has a powerful impact on the effectiveness of workers with different tasks: a south-facing desk is ideal for supportive roles; east is good for putting new ideas into practice; and southeast activates positive communication. The southwest is a classic position for a manager, as it aids consolidation and growth. On a more practical level, keeping the work space free from clutter ensures a smooth flow of ch'i around the desk.

THE LO PAN COMPASS

Above: Feng Shui masters still use the traditional lo pan compass to prescribe the locations of new buildings and decide on interior arrangements. The center contains a metal needle for locating the north pole. It is surrounded by rotatable rings containing essential information on energy patterns, planetary movements, and dates from the Chinese calendar.

Two intersecting threads cross the board, and these are used as coordinates to bring the rings into position with the compass. The lo pan contains some, or all, of the data contained on the pa kua, and these may be used as an additional tool.

Similar wisdoms:

Equivalents of ch'i (or qi) are also found in other cultures. In Japan the formative life force is known as Ki; in India as Prana; and the ancient Greek civilization knew it as Pneuma.

Feng Shui astrology

Feng Shui astrology, also known as Nine Star Ki, evolved from the trigram system and the mysterious markings on the legendary tortoise and dragon-horse. These traditions were married with a series of numbers to create the now-famous Chinese number box, said to reflect the harmony of the universe. The use of Feng Shui astrology was little known in the West until the last decades of the twentieth century, yet now it rivals other ancient forms of divination and fortune telling.

Feng Shui astrology differs from Feng Shui in that its aim is to understand the influence of time rather than space. It is about direct influences on people, not the indirect effects of buildings and external landscape. Western zodiac astrology measures the influence of the stars, whereas Feng Shui astrology gauges the interaction of heaven and earth.

Feng Shui astrology is used to gain self-awareness, assess the compatibility of relationships, and aid decision-making by suggesting how experiences may vary over time. It is also used to make geographical decisions, about changing residence, for example, or choosing an office location, or when and where to go on vacation.

The Tortoise and the Dragon-Horse

The arrangement of the nine numbers of Feng Shui astrology is derived from Chinese legend. Much of the country was submerged by a great flood, when stricken villagers reported seeing a tortoise and a horse with a dragon's head emerging from the waters. The strange markings they bore on their backs were recorded in traditional diagrams, and these were later converted into the Chinese number box. Because the numbers added in any direction always total 15, the arrangement of numbers was held to represent the principles that govern the universe.

Nine represents the highest and most active level of energy, and this is associated with the element fire; at the other extreme lies water, the least active element, and this is symbolized by the number one. The numbers are arranged in a way that expresses their intrinsic qualities and how they relate to one another. The arrangement of the numbers is known as the Magic Square. Nine is also a significant number in the Chinese calendar, which contains a nine-year cycle.

Using the Magic Square

The Magic Square is a simple arrangement of nine numerals, where each number has a specific meaning. The numbers on each line always add up to 15. Individuals may identify their own personal number according to their birth year and then seek a personalized reading from the rearranged numbers. Each year corresponds to one of the Five Elements, which has its own qualities.

Personal year 1 **Water** *individualistic, reflective*
Personal year 2 **Earth** *patient, reliable*
Personal year 3 **Tree** *enthusiastic, honest*
Personal year 4 **Tree** *sensitive, trusting*
Personal year 5 **Earth** *domineering, ambitious*
Personal year 6 **Metal** *authoritative, rational*
Personal year 7 **Metal** *optimistic, entertaining*
Personal year 8 **Earth** *determined, hardworking*
Personal year 9 **Fire** *passionate, inspirational*

To calculate your personal year number, add up the last two digits of your birth year. If their sum is less than ten, subtract it from ten to give your year number. If their sum is ten or greater, add these two digits together, then subtract their total from ten to reveal the number. For the twenty-first century add the two digits and subtract from nine. For example:

1962	**1955**	**2012**
6+2=8	5+5=10	1+2=3
10-8=2	1+0=1	9-3=6
Earth	10-1=9	**Metal**
	Fire	

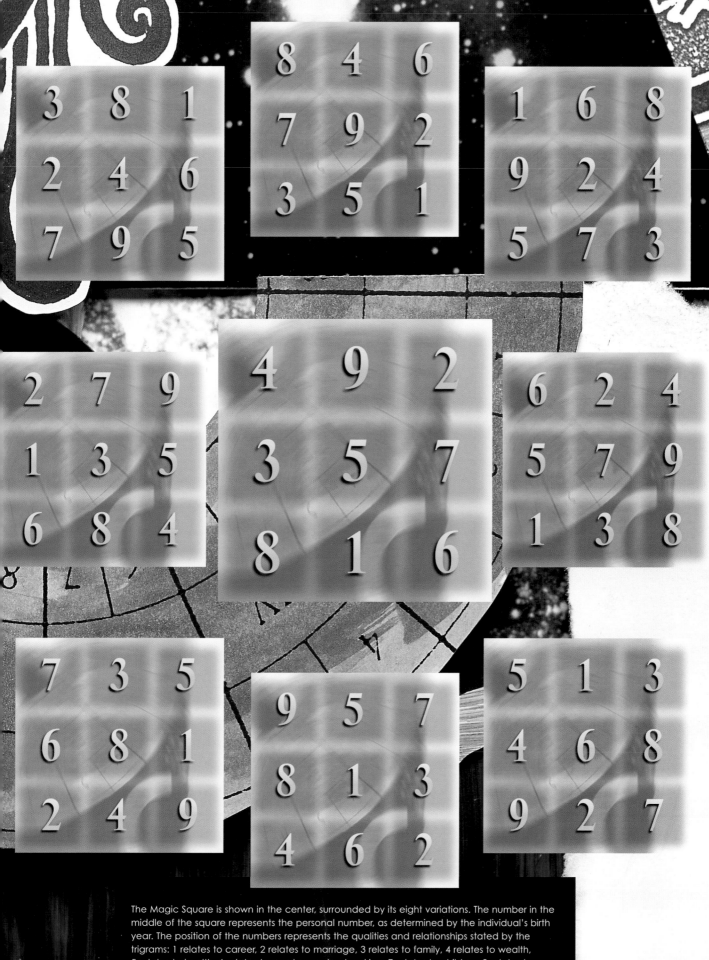

The Magic Square is shown in the center, surrounded by its eight variations. The number in the middle of the square represents the personal number, as determined by the individual's birth year. The position of the numbers represents the qualities and relationships stated by the trigrams: 1 relates to career, 2 relates to marriage, 3 relates to family, 4 relates to wealth, 5 relates to health, 6 relates to mentors and networking, 7 relates to children, 8 relates to education, and 9 relates to recognition. Each number is considered in relation to the position of this number on the central square.

Twelve animal astrology

The twelve animal system is based on the Chinese lunar calendar. It focuses on the Chinese totem animals assigned to each year, and their relationship with the ever-changing balance of energies operating at an individual's time of birth. The system has been refined through the centuries, and in the last fifty years has enjoyed increased popularity in China, Japan, and the West, offering the individual both an analysis of their personality and a tool for divination.

In twelve animal astrology, each person is assigned three animals: for their birth year (the year animal), their birth month (the lunar animal), and the animal of the time of birth (the inner animal). The information relating to each animal is used to provide an individual's full horoscope.

A strong fatalistic element developed in the later Chinese use of astrology, implying that every individual's destiny is preordained and difficult or impossible to change. This belief does not tend to feature in New Age thought, which has reinterpreted animal astrology for use in everyday life: from tastes in food to choice of vacation.

The Effect of the Five Elements

The Five Elements play a major part in animal astrology, as each animal is assigned its own sympathetic element. There are no earth animals because only four of the elements occupy a compass direction, with the earth in the center. Each year also has its own element, so the two sets of sympathies may be combined to produce 60 combinations of animal and element. The year element is always dominant, and must be seen to be in sympathy with the animal element.

ANIMAL COMPATIBILITY
Below: In the areas of friendship, love, business, and family, each animal is said to be compatible and incompatible with other animals. This chart shows the major characteristics of the twelve Chinese animals, and which should be chosen and avoided in the area of friendship.

ANIMAL CHARACTERISTICS

Animal	Characteristics	Choose	Avoid
pig	sensual, generous, eager	hare, goat, horse	snake
rat	ambitious, determined, intelligent	dragon, monkey, ox	horse
ox	patient, reliable, courageous	snake, rooster, rat	goat
tiger	daring, passionate, entertaining	horse, dragon, dog	monkey, snake
hare	intuitive, sensitive, discreet	goat, pig, dog	rat, rooster
dragon	enthusiastic, inspiring, materialistic	rat, snake, monkey	dog
snake	mysterious, sophisticated, daring	ox, rooster, dragon	pig, tiger
horse	loyal, friendly, gregarious	tiger, goat, dog	rat
goat	peaceful, adaptable, imaginative	hare, horse, pig	ox, dog
monkey	lively, quick-witted, inventive	dragon, goat, rat	tiger
rooster	courageous, protective, capable	ox, snake, dragon	hare
dog	trustworthy, responsible, sensitive	horse, tiger, hare	dragon, goat

WEST
NORTH
EAST
SOUTH
late fall
early winter
mid winter
late winter
early spring
mid-spring
late spring
early summer
midsummer
late summer
early fall
mid-fall
dog
pig
rat
ox
tiger
hare
dragon
snake
horse
goat
monkey
rooster
October
November
December
January
February
March
April
May
June
July
August
September
Lesser yang
Greater yin
Lesser yang
Greater yin
Greater yang
Lesser yin
Greater yang
Lesser yin
Greater yang
Lesser yin
Lesser yang
Greater yin
7pm-9pm
9pm-11pm
11pm-1am
1am-3am
3am-5am
5am-7am
7am-9am
9am-11am
11am-1pm
1pm-3pm
3pm-5pm
5pm-7pm
metal
water
wood
fire
earth

CHINESE ASTROLOGY AT-A-GLANCE

This chart allows you to ascertain your lunar animal from the month of birth and inner animal from the time of birth. It also indicates the yin or yang aspect for each animal and sympathetic element, both of which reveal extra characteristics of the individual.

Chinese medicine

The traditional Chinese approach to health and fitness, which involves diagnosis, treatment, and health preservation through diet and exercise, is radically different from other systems, especially modern Western medicine. It is widely used in China where it is the orthodox form of treatment for millions of people, and practiced by both privately and state-trained doctors.

Traditional Chinese Medicine, or TCM, is a practical application of more or less the same principles used throughout Chinese classical practices. It includes herbalism, acupuncture and acupressure, nutritional analysis, and specialized systems of physical exercise such as tai ch'i and dao yin. These are dealt with in turn below. TCM has had a huge impact on New Age health awareness, and indeed on mainstream Western medicine. Scientists still cannot explain, for instance, precisely how acupuncture works, but no one now seriously doubts that it does.

TCM is intrinsically holistic, concerned with the complete health of the individual. It considers the whole person – the mind, body and spirit – as well as his or her environment and social context, and seeks to change the underlying causes of a problem rather than deal merely with symptoms. It would be inconceivable in TCM, for instance, to remove any organ and expect the body somehow to work better as a result. There is strong emphasis on the early detection of health imbalances at an energetic level, before real illness develops. Subtle diagnostic methods, such as profound pulse analysis, enable this. The damaging effects of intrusive elemental factors such as damp, heat, and wind are also recognized.

Herbalism

Chinese herbalism generally relies on the use of herbs that are grown or found naturally in China. It also uses materials from animal sources, however, many of which are from other parts of the world. This has had a notoriously damaging effect on many endangered species worldwide, such as the tiger and bear, because of the great number of people being treated. As a result, it has become highly controversial.

Chinese herbalism has gained a powerful reputation in the West because of its success where Western medicine has failed, in the treatment of chronic skin conditions, for example. Multinational pharmaceutical companies are now carrying out intensive research on certain Chinese herbs that seem to be effective where their own drugs have failed, such as in the treatment of drug-resistant strains of malaria.

SELECTING THE RAW MATERIALS
Traditional medicine has continued in China during the Communist era, as illustrated by this 1973 public information poster, where the herbalist discusses the choice of herbs with his supplier. As China developed its healthcare system, conventional medicine was combined with herbal treatments at both hospital and clinic level.

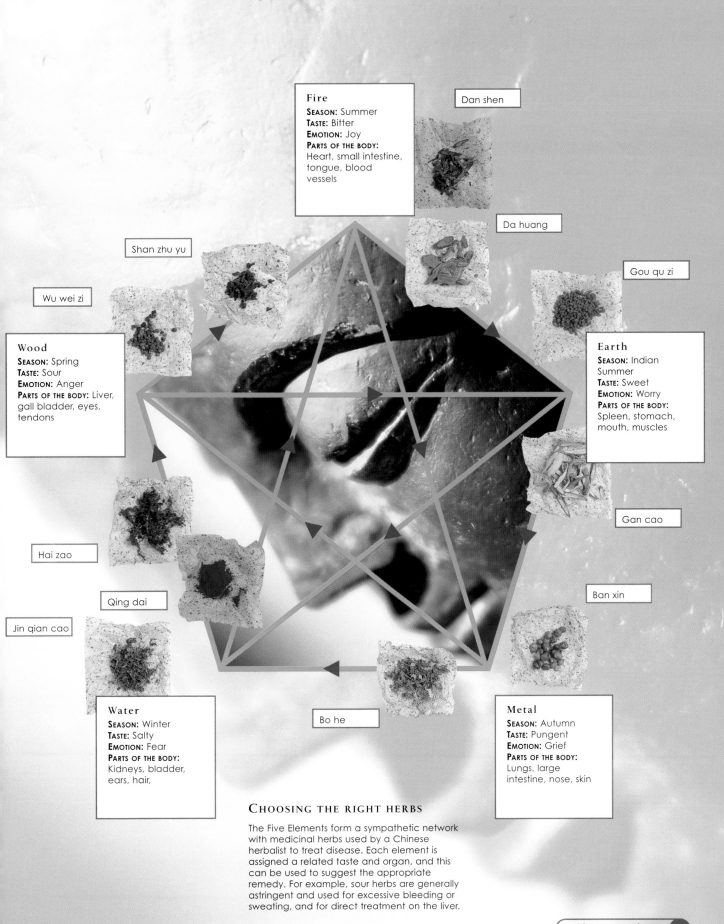

Fire
SEASON: Summer
TASTE: Bitter
EMOTION: Joy
PARTS OF THE BODY:
Heart, small intestine,
tongue, blood
vessels

Dan shen

Da huang

Shan zhu yu

Gou qu zi

Wu wei zi

Wood
SEASON: Spring
TASTE: Sour
EMOTION: Anger
PARTS OF THE BODY: Liver,
gall bladder, eyes,
tendons

Earth
SEASON: Indian
Summer
TASTE: Sweet
EMOTION: Worry
PARTS OF THE BODY:
Spleen, stomach,
mouth, muscles

Gan cao

Hai zao

Ban xin

Qing dai

Jin qian cao

Water
SEASON: Winter
TASTE: Salty
EMOTION: Fear
PARTS OF THE BODY:
Kidneys, bladder,
ears, hair,

Bo he

Metal
SEASON: Autumn
TASTE: Pungent
EMOTION: Grief
PARTS OF THE BODY:
Lungs, large
intestine, nose, skin

CHOOSING THE RIGHT HERBS

The Five Elements form a sympathetic network
with medicinal herbs used by a Chinese
herbalist to treat disease. Each element is
assigned a related taste and organ, and this
can be used to suggest the appropriate
remedy. For example, sour herbs are generally
astringent and used for excessive bleeding or
sweating, and for direct treatment on the liver.

Acupuncture

This ancient practice, involving the insertion of very fine needles into the skin at defined points to stimulate the internal flow of ch'i, is the standard form of treatment for many ailments in China. Acupuncture is claimed to be the world's oldest specific medical treatment, with origins that can be traced back to around 2500 B.C. Archaeological finds have shown that it was used in the New Stone Age, when rough needles of carved stone were used to stimulate the ch'i. Later, needles made from animal bones and bamboo took their place, until the beginnings of metalworking brought about the introduction of needles wrought from bronze, and later iron.

Acupuncture became popular in Europe in the 1930s, but it wasn't until U.S. President Nixon's visit to China in 1972 that it began to be taken seriously in the United States. It is now one of the most widely used complementary health therapies in the New Age repertoire. It combines the holistic approach of Traditional Chinese Medicine with the precise treatment of specific ailments. It has a number of specialized applications – for example, in anti-smoking therapy, and drug and alcohol rehabilitation. Acupuncture and Chinese herbalism are often used together, and many practitioners are qualified in both.

In the Chinese tradition, around 800 points on the body are linked to the organs by energy channels known as meridians. By operating on these points, acupuncture aims to restore imbalances, remove blockages, and reduce excesses in the body's internal flow of ch'i.

Acupuncture is associated with several other forms of point treatment. Moxibustion involves burning small tablets of herbal mugwort on top of the needle or warming the needle with a burning stick of compressed mugwort, thus conducting heat into the point. Cupping uses vacuum cups to create a suction effect over the points. Electro-acupuncture sends minute electrical impulses to the needles to stimulate them.

Acupressure

This is a form of massage therapy in which finger or palm pressure is used in place of needles to stimulate the points and meridians. In TCM, it is used mainly for first aid and pain relief rather than for treatment of serious illness. In New Age circles, however, it is often used as an entire treatment system, similar to shiatsu. Although acupuncture with needles is not painful, some people prefer the non-invasive form of acupressure. It is less clinical than acupuncture, and brings the added benefit of the human healing touch. It is also sometimes combined with a moxibustion stick to warm a specific area.

Treating Animals

Acupressure can be used on animals as well as humans, once the meridians have been accurately located. Moxibustion is especially effective in easing arthritic pain in older animals.

AURICULAR ACUPUNCTURE

Auricular acupuncture focuses exclusively on the ear, as this area contains so many points relating to the rest of the body. As with other acupuncture treatments, the needle is inserted a tiny way into the skin, then left to do its work. Sometimes it may be gently rotated or tapped by the practitioner to stimulate the relevant acupuncture point.

SIDE VIEW

This traditional Chinese acupuncture chart shows the positions of the meridians from a side-on view. It also displays the detailed location of points on the ear, back of the hand, foot, and side of neck.

FRONT VIEW

This face-on view of the body's acupuncture points reveals the straight linear lines of the meridians. It also shows the location of points on the tongue, around the eye, the pelvis, neck, and under the arm.

BACK VIEW

The meridian lines can once again be seen in this rear view of the body, together with the points on the top of the head, ear, and front of the hand. It also shows an internal view to remind the student which organs lie within.

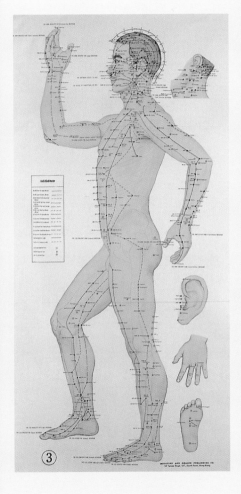

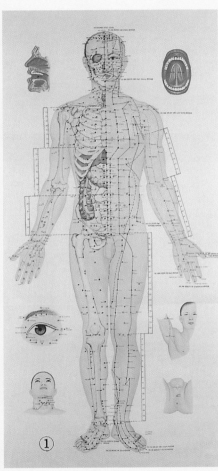

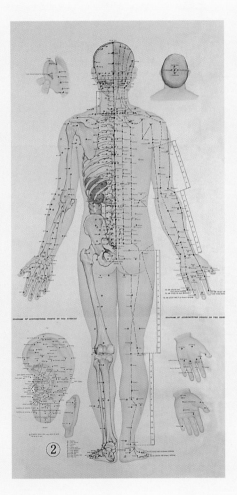

MERIDIAN LINES

Above: The 800 or so acupuncture points on the human body are divided into 12 main groups, joined together by internal meridian lines. Each meridian controls an organ, via the ch'i that flows along it. Any imbalance or blockage in the flow of ch'i affects the associated organ, causing physical or mental illness. Stimulation of the points with acupuncture needles or massage is used to revitalize the flow of ch'i, healing the organ.

Charts showing the meridian lines and acupuncture points are used in the training of TCM students to remind them of the name, location, and function of all the points.

Martial arts

Chinese martial arts are as much health regimes and spiritual disciplines as they are combat techniques. Their underlying philosophy is essentially Taoist, based on the principle that the body's energy flow provides infinitely more power than mere human strength. In practice, this involves using relaxation in action, minimum effort to attain maximum effect, and yielding instead of using force.

It is now thought that the Oriental martial arts originated in India, and were taken to China around a thousand years ago, from where they spread to Japan. They were probably first developed by monastic communities that could not use weapons, but needed some method of defending themselves.

Martial arts first appeared in the West in the early twentieth century with the introduction of the Japanese forms jujitsu and judo, and later karate, but these were treated purely as physical disciplines. However, with the New Age adoption of arts such as aikido and tai chi chuan, their original spiritual dimension has come to the fore.

Tai Chi Chuan

Tai chi chuan is often referred to as a form of moving meditation, so it may come as a surprise that it was first developed as a fighting art – indeed the name translates as "supreme ultimate fist." It was created by a thirteenth-century Taoist monk, Zhang Sanfeng, while he was studying at the Shaolin Temple. It is based on the Taoist principle that everything in the cosmos is in a state of constant flux; to stay in tune with one's surroundings, therefore, one must learn the art of harmonious change.

Tai chi chuan involves set patterns of stylized movements, through which the individual aligns his or her energies with the natural flow of ch'i in the environment. According to legend, tai chi chuan is based on the movements of animals, which were naturally in harmony with the world. The emphasis is on relaxation, concentration, balance, and the accumulation of ch'i. It is good for all-around physical and emotional health, and in dealing with stress or anxiety.

The nineteenth-century Yang style is the most widely used today, although it has been shortened for modern practice. It is popular both inside and outside China as a way of staying fit and healthy, and to complement other martial art disciplines.

Qigong

Sometimes referred to as Chinese yoga, qigong focuses on stimulating and balancing the ch'i energies in the meridian system, using postures that are generally held for some time. Emphasis is placed on the correct mental approach, on posture, and especially on breathing: control of the breath, often taken as a metaphor for ch'i, is the key to controlling the energy flow. There are many different schools, some of which involve sitting and lying down as well as standing. Practitioners believe qigong builds the immune system and wards off disease. It can be particularly effective in the treatment of chronic illness, as the intense focus on the meridian system treats the body's systems from within.

THE SINGLE WHIP SEQUENCE

Right: This four-step movement forms part of the traditional Yang style. Tai chi chuan can be practiced fast or slow, but must always be done smoothly, and with the head level.

Left: One of the most extraordinary sights to greet the visitor to modern-day China is that of large groups of young and old practicing tai chi in public spaces as communal exercise, often accompanied by recordings of traditional music.

1 Move the right hand toward the right and form a hooked hand just above shoulder height, while the left hand with the palm turned in makes an arc past your abdomen to your right shoulder.

2 Turn to the left, and take a step forward with your left foot, the heel touching the floor first.

3 Slowly rotate the left palm and push your left arm ahead at eye level. Start shifting your weight onto your left foot.

4 Bring your left arm up as your weight comes fully on your left foot. The sequence is completed.

Japan

New Agers have eagerly embraced such traditional Japanese disciplines as shiatsu, aikido, and zen, yet the country and culture still remain an enigma to many. Although Japan has been influenced by China throughout its history, and has had strong connections with other parts of eastern Asia, it still retains its own distinctive culture with unique spiritual practices.

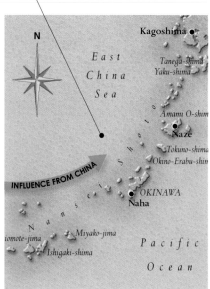

The Ryukyu islands were settled by 3000 B.C. with a mixed population from China, Japan, and Taiwan. The region shows Chinese influence with Taoist burial tombs in the shape of turtles and lion statues placed on the rooftops to ward off evil.

Acupuncture introduced to Japan by Chinese doctor Yang Er in 513 A.D. In 701 A.D., the Imperial government issued the Taiho Code, which stated that medical institutes were obliged to include courses based on "The Yellow Emperor's Classic on Acupuncture and Moxibustion."

Shamanic practices were common at the Yamato court until they were superseded by Buddhist rituals in the seventh century. Miko, or female mediums, received their gift from a divine being, either in a dream or by being possessed. Today the term miko is applied to assistants in Shinto shrines.

Amanohashidate, or the Bridge of Heaven, is said to be where two gods conceived the islands of Japan.

BUDDHISM FROM CHINA, VIA KOREA

ST. FRANCIS XAVIER, THE FIRST CHRISTIAN MISSIONARY, FROM PORTUGAL 1549.

Last stop on the 88-temple pilgrimage tour of Shikoku carried out by members of the esoteric Shingon (True Word) Buddhist sect founded in the early ninth century by Kobo Daishi. The influence of Tantric Buddhism, Hinduism, and Shinto is evident in meditation methods and temple decoration.

KEY

This key indicates the main areas of anthropological and religious significance.

 Sacred mountains

 Centers of Zen Buddhism

Shamanism was brought to Japan by Siberian tribes and developed as a means for communing with the spirits. It was practiced exclusively by women.

N

HOKKAIDO

Abashiri

Asahigawa ● ▲ *Asahi dake*
Ishikari

Otaru ● ● Kushiro
● Obihiro ●
Sapporo

Muroran ●

Osorezan, or "fearsome mountain," is known in ancient folk tales as the gathering place of dead souls. Sacred to Japanese shamans, blind female mediums known as *itako* gather here each year in July to communicate with the deceased.

● Hakodate
Tsugaru Strait
Osorezan

Aomori ●

Hirosaki ● ● Hachinohe

● Akita

Dewasanzan ▲
● Sakata
Oami ● Tsuruoka
Sadoga-shima Yamagata ● ● Sendai
● Niigata ● Fukushima
● Nagaoka ● Koriyama
J A P A N ● Iwaki
Utsunomiya ● ● Hitachi
● Takasaki ● Mito

TOKYO ■
u ● Kawasaki ● Chiba
Fujisan ▲ ● Yokohama
● Kamakura
● Shizuoka
amamatsu ●

In the search for enlightenment, ascetic Buddhist monks starve themselves before being buried alive. Mummified bodies of these "living Buddhas" can still be seen today in Buddhist temples in Oami.

P A C I F I C

O C E A N

The worship of holy mountains is an important element in the Shugendo Buddhist sect. Austere rituals, such as bathing in winter streams, are said to endow sect members with magical powers that can transform them into a Buddha.

Ancient Culture Preserved

Due to an extended period of isolation from European influence, and despite dramatic political changes in the twentieth century, Japan has retained the core of its ancient social and religious traditions. Japanese culture has fascinated visitors since it was reopened in 1868, and since then its spiritual traditions have gained wide acceptance in the West.

The earliest indigenous people were the Ainu, believed to originate in Siberia. Subsequent migrations from the south and Asia drove the Ainu into Hokkaido, the northernmost of Japan's four main islands, where only 25,000 remain today.

The dominant form of spirituality among the early tribal groups was shamanism, but with the rule of the first emperor around 600 B.C., it was gradually replaced by Shinto, which combined animism with ancestor worship. The earliest reliable records date from 400 A.D. and tell of a clan-based social order where the chief crop was rice.

Between the sixth and eighth centuries society expanded under the strong cultural influence of China: the introduction of Buddhism and Chinese-style writing led to the rapid growth of social structures and laid the foundations of the Japanese state. By the ninth century, however, the fledgling central government had collapsed as locally powerful clan chiefs refused to pay imperial taxes, and a feudal system developed characterized by almost continuous civil war.

This led in the twelfth century to the establishment of a military dictatorship under Yoritomo, who took the title of *Shogun*, and for the next 700 years, until the restoration of the emperor in 1868, Japan was ruled by warriors. This was the period of the Samurai, a professional warrior class who lived by the code of *bushido*, which formalized Zen and Confucian ideas of loyalty, personal honor, and self-sacrifice.

In the twentieth century, Japan became a major economic power, acting as a model for other Asian economies. Its most influential contributions to the New Age include Zen Buddhism, specialized arts such as aikido and the tea ceremony, and the healing practices of shiatsu and reiki. Japan has contributed to the New Age peace movement through its unenviable distinction of being the only country to experience and suffer the effects of the nuclear bomb.

Early Spirituality

The early spirituality of Japan had much in common with shamanistic cultures elsewhere. Practices included animism, or the worship of nature spirits; journeying to the Otherworld; and the use of altered states of consciousness for healing and divination. Japanese shamans wore cloaks decorated with stuffed snakes and caps of owl or eagle feathers, highlighting the fundamental interaction with the natural world.

Shamanism profoundly influenced later spiritual development in Japan, especially that of Shinto. Indeed, shamans were a common feature of society until the seventh century when shamanism was downgraded to the level of folk religion. Today, Japan's shamanistic heritage is evident in the blind female *itako* of northern Japan who act as mediums for ancestral spirits. Modern counterparts can also be found among the founders of Japan's so-called "new religions." Miki Nakayama, for example, set up the Tenrikyo religion after claiming to have heard a divine voice.

Shinto

Shinto, or the "Way of the Gods," is commonly described as ancestor-worship, but as so often the full story is a little more complex than that. It developed from early shamanistic roots to become the state religion of Japan, and has lasted right into the modern era. When Shinto was embraced by the early emperors, they claimed divinity through direct lineage back to the Sun Goddess. The concept of the emperor-as-god was not officially abandoned until after World War II.

The basis of traditional Shinto was the acknowledgment of different forms of *kami* or divine energy, such as that of ancestors, local spirits, or the sun. The goal of Shinto was to unite people with these spirit energies, in order to foster communal harmony, healing, and abundance. The energies were also consulted in divination rites. As in many ancient societies, annual festivals were based around the natural year, especially the sowing in spring and harvesting in autumn.

Shinto has been influenced by many other spiritual traditions over the years, including Chinese Buddhism and Confucianism, and is still a thriving religion. Many modern Japanese people still believe in the power of ancestors and natural spirits, regardless of the faith they now profess.

Between the sixteenth and nineteenth centuries, a distinctive form of esoteric mysticism called Shugendo developed in the mountains among ascetics and hermits. It emphasized magic-religious power, and was based on a blend of folk Shinto, esoteric Buddhism, and Taoist magic. The movement represented a revival of the teachings of the legendary shaman En-no-Gyoja, who lived in the eighth century, and its influence has extended into modern times.

MESSAGE TO THE GODS

Invoking the Shinto gods for protection from bad luck or for help in achieving an objective is still a common practice in modern Japan. Japanese people buy these simple wooden *ema*, or votive offerings, write their prayer on the back, and then tie them in a conspicuous place in the shrine precincts.

Zen Buddhism

Zen, in the eyes of the West perhaps the archetypal Oriental religious tradition, originated in China as a result of the encounter between Buddhism and indigenous Taoist beliefs. Ch'an, as it was known, found ready acceptance in Japan, where it took on the localized name Zen. It came to have a profound influence on all aspects of art and culture, in particular on flower arranging, garden design, and the tea ceremony.

Buddhism was introduced to Japan from China via Korea in the sixth century, and gradually took root in Japanese spirituality. A variety of sects developed in a distinctly Japanese vein. Some of these still thrive today, such as Nichiren Buddhism, which began in the thirteenth century and has now spread to more than 100 other countries.

In the twelfth century, two Japanese monks, Eisai and Dogen, went to China to study a particular form of Buddhism called Ch'an, known for its emphasis on spontaneity. These two priests are now recognized as the founders of the two major Japanese Zen sects, Rinzai and Soto. Eisai taught a way of enlightenment through the contemplation of enigmatic

questions or puzzles known as *koans*. These were designed to throw the seeker into a mental dilemma that could lead to a spontaneous flash of insight.

Dogen offered a way of enlightenment through *zazen* or seated meditation, in which the practitioner seeks to attain a higher level of consciousness by emptying his or her mind of conscious thought. At a traditional zazen session, a roving supervisor encourages mental concentration by striking the shoulders of anyone who dozes off with a stick. These two strands formed the core of Zen Buddhism.

In Japan, as elsewhere, one of the functions of communal religion was to unite people. But the Zen philosophers

Celebrated Koan

What is the sound of one hand clapping? If a tree should fall in the forest with no one to hear it, what noise does it make?

believed that rigid codes of behavior and formalized Buddhist and Shinto ritual created a barrier to personal enlightenment. They sought to disintegrate formal habits of thought and replace them with a more direct perception of reality, in which action was preferred to study.

Zen and the New Age

The spread of Zen had an enormous influence on many facets of everyday life in Japan; simple, elemental, and undecorated designs for buildings, interiors, and gardens became the norm. The idea of reaching enlightenment through mastery of technique contributed to the development of other disciplines.

Zen has continued to thrive in the modern era, and has attracted a strong following outside Japan, especially in North America. It has been a source of inspiration for artists, poets, and musicians since its popularization by Jack Kerouac and the Beat Generation in the 1950s. Buddhist teachings also spread to Europe, on the wave of New Age enthusiasm for spirituality.

THE TAMING OF THE BULL

Right: Zen monks used ink paintings to explain complex Zen themes such as *satori*, or enlightenment. The vitality and humor of many of the great Zen monks, such as Hakuin, is reflected in their paintings and calligraphy. The Taming of the Bull is a renowned sequence of illustrations showing the path to enlightenment. It was copied from the original Chinese drawings by Shubun, a Japanese Zen painter-monk. In the story, the bull represents the spirit, and the herdsman the person engaged in meditation. In illustrations one and two, the herdsman struggles to tame the bull. In illustrations three and four, the bull gradually submits to his control. In illustrations five, six, and seven, the bull is tethered and the herdsman is at peace with himself. In illustrations eight and nine, he recognizes the symbolism of the bull and lets it go. The bull vanishes. In the final illustration, the herdsman reaches enlightenment and feels at one with the universe.

SEVENTH ILLUSTRATION
The herdsman at peace after his meditation.

NINTH ILLUSTRATION
Equilibrium is restored.

Zen and the art of living

Practicing highly stylized formal traditions, such as the tea ceremony, was seen as a means of developing a deepening awareness of Zen ideas. Simplicity and unselfconsciousness have elevated these traditional pursuits to exquisite art forms.

Living Zen

Ideas based on Zen permeated Japanese society and education, partly because Zen philosophy was embraced by the ruling samurai, or warrior, class. The emphasis on direct action, spontaneity, selflessness, and personal enlightenment, together with the rigorous spiritual and physical demands, particularly appealed to samurai, already accustomed to military discipline. For the samurai, the simple ritual of the tea ceremony offered an escape from military concerns into a world of reverence, poetry, and harmony with nature. Shogun

Yoshimasa's patronage of the tea ceremony in the mid-fifteenth century led to increasing Zen influence on related arts such as ikebana (flower arranging), ink painting, and garden design.

The Zen tenets of simplicity, spontaneity, and mindfulness of each moment have found deep resonance among New Agers. Key to the popularity of Zen in the West was the work in English of Daisetz Suzuki (1877–1966) and the publication of Robert Pirsig's *Zen and the Art of Motorcycle Maintenance* in 1975.

THE WAY OF TEA

The host presents a bowl of tea with smooth unselfconscious movements according to the strict rituals of the tea ceremony. Although originally practiced by Zen monks and later refined by wealthy merchants, today the ceremony is largely performed by women.

The Tea Ceremony

The tea ceremony, or *chado*, is an example of the application of Zen to ordinary life. The word *do* means "way," as in kendo (Japanese fencing) and karate-do ("the way of the empty hand"), suggesting an element of spiritual transformation.

Chado is now 400 years old. It is a uniquely Japanese application of Buddhist principles, based around the simple task of making a bowl of tea for guests. It transforms this everyday activity into an elaborate training exercise. There are formal procedures for the arrival of guests, entry into the tea-room, exchanging greetings, boiling the water, making and serving the tea, and for farewells. The ceremony can last for four hours. Every action is invested with total attention or "mindfulness," for guests as well as the host.

Emphasis is placed on creating an attitude of alert tranquility and fluid movements through self-control and self-awareness. There is great attention to detail in the creation of an orderly and harmonious setting and an aesthetic and meditative atmosphere. The air of reverence is emphasized by the simplicity of the surroundings. Ultimately, the goal is to develop people's physical, emotional, and spiritual resources so that the self can be transcended.

Ikebana

Ikebana, or kado, the "way of flowers," was also seen as a vehicle for natural expression, and an attempt in the Zen tradition to break the chain of conventional logic and so make possible a flash of enlightenment. The art of ikebana developed from the ritual flower arrangements offered at Buddhist temples, and formal style rules were first laid down in the seventh century. Ikebana was further refined in the sixteenth century by Sen no Rikyu, who, influenced by Zen ideas of simplicity, introduced basic implements such as rustic flower holders, ladles and whisks made from bamboo, and roughcast black teabowls. He was also responsible for introducing smaller teahouses, which forced samurai warriors to leave their swords outside before entering the peaceful and harmonious atmosphere of the tea ceremony.

The sudden insights that ikebana can offer are well illustrated in the story of a shogun (military governor) who went to the garden of the tea ceremony master Sen no Rikyu after hearing reports of a fabulous display of morning glories in full bloom. To his dismay he found that they had all been cut down and he entered the tea house with sword drawn, fully intent on venting his anger. But he stopped in his tracks, for there in the alcove was one stem with a perfect blossom. In that moment, he understood the power of ikebana to teach the sudden and spontaneous nature of enlightenment.

THE WAY OF FLOWERS

Top right: Ikebana portrays the relationship between heaven (the tall center stem), man (medium stem), and earth (short stem).

Right: A widespread Zen activity since the fourteenth century, ikebana is still popular today. It has been rediscovered by the New Age Movement as a vital form of visual expression and meditation.

Healing therapies

A number of Japanese healing techniques have recently become popular in the West. Shiatsu, a type of massage using the fingers, palms, elbows, knees, and feet, effectively alleviates functional and stress-related problems.

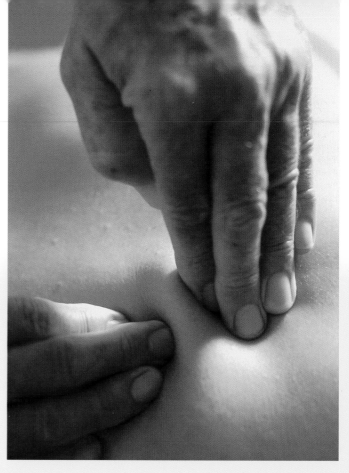

Shiatsu

The word shiatsu literally means "finger pressure." As a professional therapy it is relatively new, but its origins stretch back to Japanese folk medicine, and the traditional use of pressure-based treatment in the home. In ancient times, family members would use shiatsu to bring relief and healing to other family members, in combination with local herbs and other folk wisdom. Mothers would teach what they knew to their daughters, thus ensuring that the knowledge was passed on from generation to generation. Even today, shiatsu and acupuncture (*hari*) are commonly used to treat day-to-day ills.

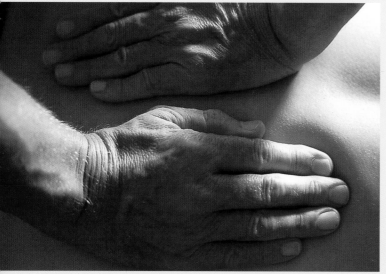

Shiatsu was developed to a higher level of sophistication in order to treat specific and more severe illnesses. In this form, it became the more or less automatic career option for anyone who was blind, and was known as *anma*. In the 1920s, *anma* was merged with the principles of traditional Chinese medicine and Western physiology, and modern therapeutic shiatsu was born. In 1964 shiatsu was established as a professional treatment in Japan.

Shiatsu is primarily concerned with correcting the body's internal flow of energy or *ki*. As in acupuncture, this energy runs in channels known as meridians; its flow may become

1 The hands are laid gently over the eyes.   **2** The hands are rested ge

ACUPUNCTURE WITHOUT NEEDLES
Left: Shiatsu can be performed in two ways.
The practioner may stimulate specific pressure
points, or *tsubo*, with his fingertips to regulate
the flow of ki throughout the body (opposite).
Alternatively, the palms may be used to
massage the body to stimulate the flow of ki
(below left).

blocked, or may be deficient in some parts of the body and excessive in others.

With its deep, pressure-point approach, shiatsu produces a more profound effect than regular massage techniques, benefiting the mind and emotions as well as the body. For many clients, being treated while clothed is also a plus factor.

Shiatsu is one of the fastest growing New Age health therapies. In the 1980s, it was embraced by many international celebrities, including Princess Diana, which greatly enhanced its popularity.

Reiki

Reiki is a form of spiritual healing that was developed in Japan early in the twentieth century by Dr. Mikao Usui. Recently, a number of different methods have evolved in addition to the Usui system, such as Karuna reiki and Tera-mai, which makes use of the four elements, fire, water, earth, and air.

In reiki practice, energy is transferred to the recipient by laying the hands on or near the body, to promote healing and well-being, and to alleviate stress. Becoming a practitioner in reiki requires initiation or "attunement" into a system of secret symbols that are believed to empower the process of healing. Ancient Egyptian and Mayan symbols have recently been added to this system.

Today, reiki is extremely popular in the West; it has more practitioner-training courses competing for customers than any other healing therapy.

LAYING ON HANDS

Below: Applying reiki can induce a deep feeling of relaxation in the recipient. The practitioner will generally start at the top of the body, as shown here, and then move on to the pelvic area and legs, repeating the process on the recipient's back. This powerful tool may also unleash emotional traumas that may have been buried in the subconscious for years. For this reason, it is important to allow a period of peaceful reflection after a reiki session.

3 The practitioner raises the head and places the hands underneath.

4 The hands are placed lightly on the collarbone.

5 The hands are placed on the chest.

AUSTRALASIA & THE PACIFIC

Stretched out along the Pacific Rim, some of the world's oldest examples of primal spiritual belief have survived, preserved as a result of the area's isolation from the rest of civilization. Australia, in particular, is home to the planet's strongest links with the Stone Age, its indigenous culture featuring a shamanistic spiritual system that is totally integrated with practical life.

Australasia and the Pacific

Australia and the island groups of the Pacific – Melanesia, Micronesia, and Polynesia – were settled from East Asia. These migrations were separated by tens of thousands of years, but despite this, the cultures share elements of a rich spiritual history and sophisticated tribal folklore.

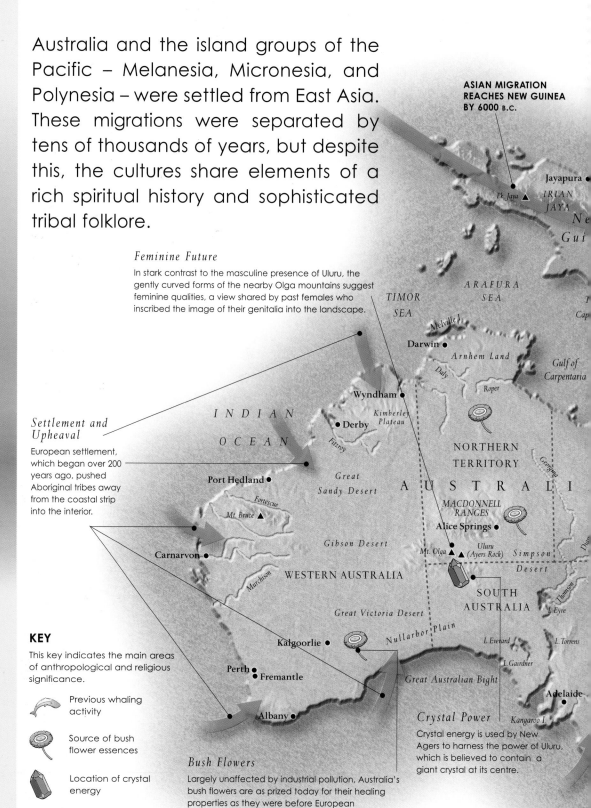

ASIAN MIGRATION REACHES NEW GUINEA BY 6000 B.C.

Feminine Future

In stark contrast to the masculine presence of Uluru, the gently curved forms of the nearby Olga mountains suggest feminine qualities, a view shared by past females who inscribed the image of their genitalia into the landscape.

Settlement and Upheaval

European settlement, which began over 200 years ago, pushed Aboriginal tribes away from the coastal strip into the interior.

KEY

This key indicates the main areas of anthropological and religious significance.

- Previous whaling activity
- Source of bush flower essences
- Location of crystal energy

Bush Flowers

Largely unaffected by industrial pollution, Australia's bush flowers are as prized today for their healing properties as they were before European settlement. Many are now grown commercially for the alternative health market.

Crystal Power

Crystal energy is used by New Agers to harness the power of Uluru, which is believed to contain a giant crystal at its centre.

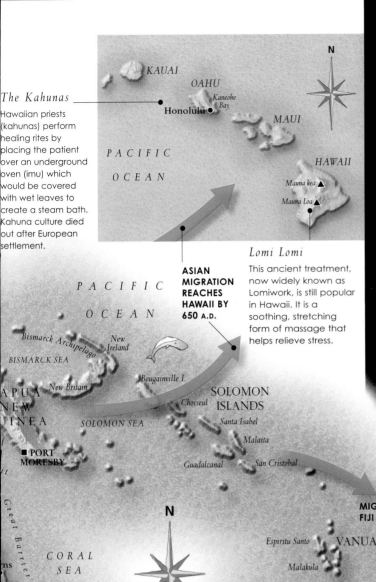

The Kahunas
Hawaiian priests (kahunas) perform healing rites by placing the patient over an underground oven (imu) which would be covered with wet leaves to create a steam bath. Kahuna culture died out after European settlement.

ASIAN MIGRATION REACHES HAWAII BY 650 A.D.

Lomi Lomi
This ancient treatment, now widely known as Lomiwork, is still popular in Hawaii. It is a soothing, stretching form of massage that helps relieve stress.

MIGRATION REACHES FIJI BY 3500 B.C.

MIGRATION SPREADS TO EASTER ISLAND BY 400 A.D.

Saving the Reef
In 1979 the Australian government ordered a ban on petroleum exploration in waters surrounding the Great Barrier Reef.

EUROPEAN SETTLERS LAND HERE

MIGRATION REACHES NEW ZEALAND BY 750 A.D.

Harmonic Convergence
José Arguelles' 1987 theory of cosmic forces predicted a shift from tribal to planetary consciousness. This was celebrated by attempts to form a human chain around Uluru, and the drawing of the Rainbow Serpent at Bronte Beach, Sydney.

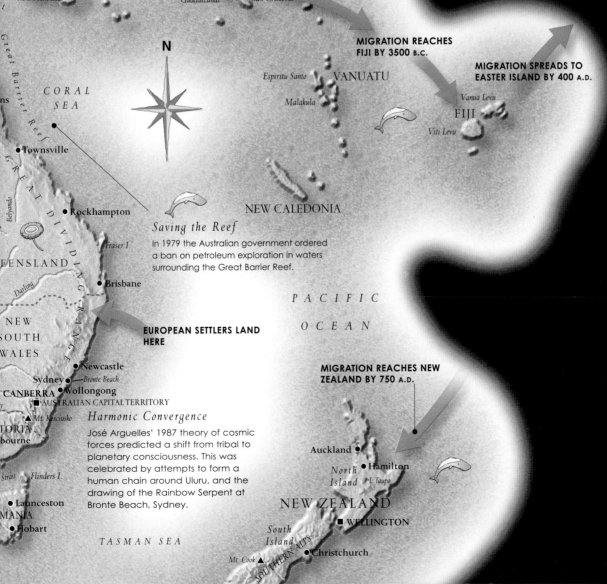

Aboriginal spirituality, in particular the concept of Dreamtime and the use of flower medicine, has strongly influenced New Age thinking, These traditions were almost destroyed by European colonization, but are now gaining acceptance throughout the New Age Movement.

Aboriginal Australia

The vast, empty spaces of the Australian landscape were once home to over five hundred ethnic subgroups of Aboriginal culture. These earliest inhabitants are thought to have migrated in two main waves from Asia – dark-skinned Aborigines are related to ethnic groups in south India and Sri Lanka. This occurred during the last Ice Age, when sea levels were lowest, and great land bridges connected the largest islands of southeast Asia, making the expanses of ocean relatively easy to cross.

Spiritual elements from this time can still be found in Aboriginal culture: despite European colonization, much about their way of life has not changed for over 35,000 years.

Spiritual traditions

In Australian Aboriginal culture, life is a continuous ritual. Central to this is Dreamtime, which forms the basis of all spiritual activity. Dreamtime is both a representation of the mythical past, and also part of the ongoing present. In dream mythology, spirit beings shaped the land; humans then came into existence, and established rituals to ensure the continuity of creation.

Every individual has a special Dreamtime ancestor, associated with a particular element of the natural world, such as an animal or plant. This becomes his or her personal totem or *kobong*, and he or she must never harm or kill that species.

Connection to the land is a key element of Aboriginal spirituality. The land is regarded as a living being: if human Dreamtime activity ceases, the land dies. Certain places are particularly sacred, such as Uluru (Ayers Rock) in Australia's Northern Territory, which is thought to be the earth's navel.

Aboriginal art, best known for its paintings on bark and rock, is closely linked with religion. The rock paintings are perpetually repainted, and some date back 15,000 years. They depict humans, animals, and spirits that may be represented as geometric shapes. Unique features include x-ray-style paintings that show inner organs, representing shamanic visions, and dot paintings that depict dreams. Aboriginal art is now highly prized in the international art market.

The Aboriginal shaman is called Karadji or Mekigar, meaning "clever man." He uses a state of trance to journey to the Otherworld, to communicate with spirits, and to cure illness. The Karadji initiation is an arduous process that involves symbolic death and rebirth.

CROSSING THE CULTURE GAP
Animal motifs dominate native culture, and have fed back into European Australian culture, as shown by this contemporary flooring design (left).

SPIRIT OF PLACE
Aborigine cave paintings of man, animal, and sky illustrate the unbroken link between native cultures and their physical environment (right).

DEATH AND SURVIVAL

Right: Crocodiles shared the wild outback with native Aborigines, and became part of the individual's Dreamtime legend.

Divination features strongly in Aboriginal culture, and is obtained by entering Dreamtime. The purpose of divination here, however, is to help individuals align themselves with the spirit energies in order to create a propitious future, rather than simply to predict events. Crystals, rocks, and pebbles, living expressions of spirit, are used as "Wild Stones," objects of power that are thrown for the purpose of divination. Each individual also possesses a churinga, a specially carved wooden totemic object. A number of New Age oracles have been based on these traditional practices.

Death forms an important focus in Aboriginal awareness. It is not regarded as the end, but as "survival in infinity," and it is essential to prepare for it correctly. When an individual senses that death is near, he or she goes alone into the mountains to engage in preparatory mystical practices, such as meditating or sky-gazing, in readiness for the next stage of the journey.

Bush flower essences

For generations, Australian aborigines have passed down the oral tradition of bush medicine, and a wide range of plants is used to treat physical and emotional ailments. Some of these treatments are in the form of Bush flower essences, the concentrated dew from the flowers of certain healing plants.

Bush flower essences have received widespread publicity and, with increasing commercial demand, many of the flowers are now grown in controlled environments, so the concentrated essences can be manufactured for the general market. The Aborigine tradition of eating bush flowers varied according to which plants were available and the reason for their prescription. Often the plant and the flower were eaten together to gain the maximum nutritional benefit. Sometimes the flower was eaten alone for its nectar content or medicinal qualities, or in the case of a poisonous plant, people would sit on a clump of the flower to absorb its healing vibration.

The quantity of flowers available in the Australian bush is highly dependent on the amount of rainfall, and there are also wide regional variations. The spring rains prompt an explosion of floral growth, and the colorful bush flowers come into bloom almost immediately.

The Australian aborigines' practice of using plants for healing is extremely old, with a strong emphasis on treating spiritual and emotional ailments. Australia has both the world's oldest and the greatest number of flowering plants, displaying striking color and ancient forms. It is also a relatively unpolluted source of plant material. As a result, Australian Bush flower essences have become extremely sought-after throughout the world.

Flower Essences Today

The 50 most effective flower essences have been identified for common usage, and these are now sold in health stores for personal use. Flower essences are not directly prescribed for physical ailments, as natural health practitioners believe many physical symptoms are often a manifestation of emotional imbalances. The threat of extinction faced by many Australian wild flowers has resulted in a concerted effort to preserve them in the wild, and "in captivity" in controlled growing

COMMERCIAL POTENTIAL

There is a growing demand for flower essences, such as camomile (shown below). These essences offer the flower's medicinal properties in a much less concentrated form than the essential oils used in aromatherapy.

FEMALE FLOWERS
Practitioners believe that Wisteria flower essence is useful for women who feel uncomfortable about their sexuality. It helps resolve negative feelings about intimacy and past sexual traumas.

environments. This movement is in harmony with renewed interest in flower essence medicine, as practitioners now have access to many of the flowers for the first time.

Flower essences differ from other medicines in that they do not contain active chemical substances, in much the same way as homeopathic remedies are so dilute that they do not contain any measureable quantities of the constituents of the original source. Indeed, our understanding of the way they work is very incomplete. Described as "liquid energy," it is thought that the essence contains the vibrational energies of the flower, and that this is capable of subtly but powerfully affecting the recipient's own life forces. Because of their extremely low concentrations, they are free from side-effects, safe for anyone to use, and adjust to the needs of the individual taking them. If an inappropriate remedy is chosen, it simply will not work.

The principal effect of flower essences is a realigning of the emotions, thus enabling the individual to move on from a distressing situation, or the dispersion of a harmful belief. Each plant species relates to a particular negative emotion, and promotes its positive counterpart. For instance, essence of gentian is related to despondency, and larch promotes self-confidence. Flower essences can be extracted from an extremely wide range of flora, from common wildflowers and so-called weeds to alpine flowers, exotic orchids, and tree blossoms. There are flower essences from the Amazon rainforests, the Himalayas, the Arizona desert, the Alaskan wilderness, and the Scottish New Age center of Findhorn, among many others. As with aromatherapy, flower essences are often combined to provide a complete treatment.

Wisteria – A New Flower Essence

Wisteria (*Wisteria sinensis*) is an excellent example of how the tradition of bush flower essences has been reinterpreted by the New Age. Wisteria is not native to Australia, but was introduced by European settlers in the nineteenth century. The essence from the lilac-colored petals is used to treat female sexual ailments.

New Zealand and the Pacific Islands

The island chains of Polynesia, Melanesia, and Micronesia stretch out in wide arcs to the northeast and northwest of New Zealand over a vast area of the South Pacific prone to geological shifts and volcanic activity. The indigenous spiritual traditions are based on the worship of ancestors and supernatural beings. Animals, reptiles, and fish are viewed as totems, and magic and sorcery are widely practiced.

RITUAL DANCING, COOK ISLANDS, POLYNESIA
Polynesian tribes include the universal figures of shaman priests, medicine men, and village elders. On major festivals and religious holidays, celebratory dancing is performed to honor religious deities.

New Zealand's North and South Islands were first colonized by Polynesian islanders around 750 A.D. — legend tells that the first settlers arrived in seven canoes. The Maori language of their descendants is closely related to Hawaiian, Tahitian, and other languages of the area east of Samoa, and their culture is based on seagoing activities and, at one time, frequent tribal warfare.

Spiritual Traditions

In Maori mythology, there are three realms of creation. The original realm of nothingness has the power to produce the other worlds. The world of night is the world of the gods and ancestors. The world of light is inhabited by humans. Communication is possible between these worlds through shamanistic means.

The main shamanic figure is the *tohunga* who is a priest, seer and expert in magic. He uses a variety of methods. One is "second sight," known as *matakite*. Another is the interpretation of natural omens, or *aitua* — the falling of marked sticks and leaves, and weather patterns. A divination method called *Niu Kowhata* involves the casting of stones and shells. Kite-flying is also used as an oracle — a practice that is totally unique to the Maoris. Another form of diviner is the *kuia*, an elderly woman who is consulted for the interpretation of dreams. Nowadays, some kuias use their skills to predict winners in horse races.

Many of these methods were originally used in planning for battle or war. No important venture would be undertaken without obtaining a spiritual blessing. Sacred ancestral objects possessed the power to grant this blessing, known as *mana*.

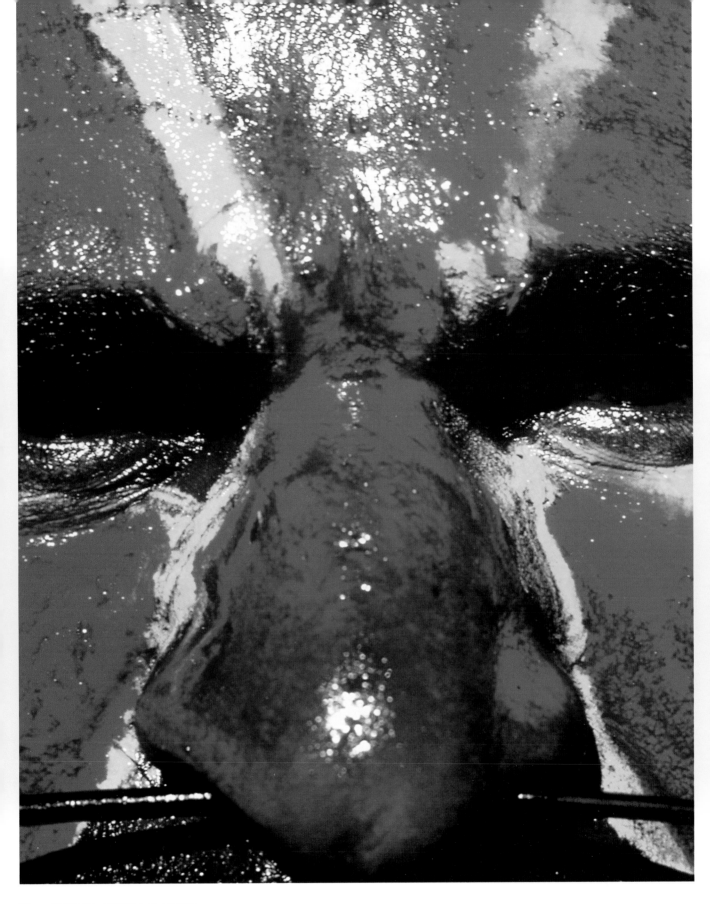

NEW GUINEA RITUAL DANCER
In the New Age era, these exuberant lords of the dance, with their exotic face decoration, command a newfound respect among more sedate Western societies.

THE EYE OF KANALOA

Left: According to Kahuna legend, this ancient symbol radiates energies that promote happiness and good fortune.

IAO NEEDLE PEAK, HAWAII

Far left: In the islands' mountain fastnesses, their people's ancient practices still survive, despite near obliteration by nineteenth-century missionaries.

The Huna of Hawaii

Horrified by what they saw as idol-worship, and fearful of reports of human sacrifice, European missionaries made a determined effort to stamp out the islanders' shamanistic tradition. Modern healers are now reviving some of its underrated practices.

Huna is the ancient shamanistic religion of the Hawaiian Islands. When Christian missionaries arrived in the 1820s, it was outlawed and suppressed almost to the point of obliteration. However, in the twentieth century, investigators such as Max Freedom Long realized that Huna contains a very potent system of ancient magic, based on a highly sophisticated model of the human psyche. The *Kahunas* – doctor-priest-teacher-practitioners or "Keepers of the Secret" – were able to cure the sick, develop immunity to fire, predict and influence the future, and even raise the dead. Now, the shamanistic practices of Huna are becoming increasingly well-

RHYTHM IS ALL

Right: Hawaiian Hula dancers show how to let the life force flow.

known, and are widely used in the fields of modern healing, psychology, and personal transformation.

Contemporary uses of Huna principles include:

● Kupono counselling, a way of resolving conflict and harmonizing relationships. It can be used by individuals, groups, or organizations.

● Shamanistic healing, using a variety of methods, including soul retrieval, energy clearing, the healing use of sound, and extracting illness with the spirits of plants.

● Personal Power, which seeks to emphasize the cooperative and loving nature of the adventurer, rather than the more adversarial way of the warrior.

● Kahi Loa, a massage system based on the seven Hawaiian elements. Its effect is to promote a free and abundant flow of life force through the body.

HAWAIIAN STATUES

These sophisticated models of the human psyche provide a strong and powerful image of native deities. Animal totems are also made as communal talismans.

Glossary

A

ACUPUNCTURE: Ancient Chinese use of fine needles to harmonise flow of ch'i throughout the body. It is based on a complex map of the body and the channels, or meridians, along which the ch'i travels. Its benefits are now widely recognized in the West, where its popularization owes much to the New Age movement.

AROMATHERAPY: The use of essential oils in healing, closely allied to therapeutic massage. Although formally started in the twentieth century, it draws on knowledge of essential oils that goes back several thousand years, particularly to Ancient Egypt.

AURA: An electro-magnetic field that surrounds the human form and which can now be diagnostically scanned thanks to modern photographic techniques.

B

BHAGAVAD-GITA: The classical Hindu text that expounds the doctrine of reincarnation.

BRAHMA: The creator of the universe in Hindu theology.

BUDDHISM: Multi-disciplinary religion that preaches the way to enlightenment through self-discipline and meditation. It has an estimated 200 million adherents worldwide, including growing numbers in the West, but its main strongholds are in China, Japan, eastern Asia, Sri Lanka, Tibet, and in Nepal, where it originated in the sixth century B.C.

C

CABALA: Esoteric Jewish methodology for interpreting the hidden meanings of the Hebrew scriptures, claimed to be handed down by oral tradition. New Age Cabala provides a secular form of the original teachings.

D

DOWSING: Also known as water divining – a popular folk method of seeking springs or mineral deposits, in which the dowser explores the ground holding a witch-hazel twig or other light instrument which reacts by jerking to the vibration of the underground water.

E

ENNEAGRAM: A graphic device used by Moslem Sufi mystics for understanding the cosmos and reading a person's character.

F

FENG SHUI: The Chinese study of the energy of place, literally meaning "wind and water." Used routinely in Chinese communities to plan the layout of homes and the location of buildings. Increasingly practiced in the West.

FIVE ELEMENTS: Wood, Fire, Earth, Metal, and Water. Key concepts in Chinese cosmology, commonly used in the practice of Feng Shui and Chinese astrology.

I

I CHING: The Book of Days, the classical Chinese treatise on anticipating future events.

K

KARATE DO: A form of Japanese unarmed combat, influenced by Zen Buddhism.

KARMA: The Hindu doctrine on the retributive link between an individual's behaviour and the process of reincarnation and migration of the soul.

KENDO: A style of Japanese fencing, influenced by the teachings of Zen Buddhism.

L

LEY LINES: Spiritual power lines believed to follow the lie of the land and to connect places or buildings containing high charges of spiritual energy. Particularly numerous in Europe.

M

MANTRA: A word or phrase that influences the mind through incessant repetition. Used widely in Buddhism and Hinduism.

MANDALA: A graphic diagram that aids Buddhist or Hindu contemplation.

O

OGHAM STICKS: Marked twigs used by Druids to assist them in divination.

P

PA KUA: A diagrammatic tool used in the Feng Shui analysis of an interior, building, or location.

PRANA: A Hindu term for life force, corresponding to the Chinese term ch'i.

Q

QIGONG: The Chinese system of breathing, posture control, and mental equilibrium, used to consolidate inner and outer peace and strength.

R

RAYMI: The Inca festival of the sun god.

REIKI: A non-invasive healing system developed in Japan in the early twentieth century.

RUNE: An ancient process of divination using stone inscriptions. Practiced in northwestern Europe.

S

SHAMAN: A priest, originally of the native tribes of Siberia. The term is now generally used for spiritual practitioners worldwide.

SHIATSU: A Japanese form of therapeutic massage applied to the acupuncture pressure points.

SHINTO: The state religion of Japan, predating the arrival of Buddhism and still widely followed. It stresses reverence for ancestors and, until the Second World War, the Emperor of Japan.

SHIVA: One of Hinduism's principal deities.

SMUDGING: The use by Native Americans of smoke from burning herbs to banish negative vibrations from persons or places.

SUFISM: The ecstatic mystical movement within the Islam faith.

T

TAI CHI CHUAN: Stylized movements based on Chinese martial arts to improve wellbeing.

TAOISM: One of the three main strands of Chinese spirituality, codified by Lao Tzu 2700 years ago.

TALISMAN: An object credited with power to benefit its wearer or owner.

TANTRA: The esoteric Hindu and Buddhist tradition of ritual yoga to raise spiritual awareness.

TAROT: A system of illustrated cards, devised in fourteenth century Italy for the purposes of divination.

TASSEOMANCY: Tea-leaf reading to foretell the future.

U

UPANISHADS: Sanskrit writings of a theosophical and philosophical character attached to the Veda, the holy books of Hinduism.

V

VISHNU: One of Hinduism's principal deities.

VISION QUEST: A character-building initiation rite of a native American male, in which he wanders for several days in the wilderness.

VEDA: The four sacred books of Hinduism.

Y

YOGA: A system of enhancing awareness by physical posture and breathing. It is based on a Hindu philosophy showing the means of freeing the soul from migration.

Z

ZEN: A Chinese fusion of Buddhism and native Taoist beliefs, which acquired its biggest following in Japan. Zen stresses meditation and has inspired rituals such as the Japanese tea ceremony and flower arranging.

ZOROASTRIANISM: Ancient Persian religion, founded by the prophet Zoroaster, and known for its veneration of fire. Spread to India, where its adherents are called Parsis.

Index

Credits

Heather Angel 27br
Bo-Giraudon 126
Bridgeman-Giraudon 68, 69
CFCL/Image Select 164b
J-L Charmet 94t, 106, 127, 148b, 160
Clark/Clinch 13, 22l, 41, 89t, 124, 135 (tr&bl), 138l, 139
Sylvia Corday 13, 47br, 83tr, 119, 121, 122
Duchas, The Heritage Service 55b
E.T. Archive 8b, 32c, 60t, 61(t&b), 64, 77, 79r, 81, 82b, 85b, 88b, 93, 117, 146b
Feng Shui for Modern Living Magazine 155
Flowers & Foliage/Ashton 183
Government of Hyderabad, Pakistan/Image Select 119
Image Bank 2, 9r, 12, 13, 14, 15, 18 (t&b), 21, 22br, 23t, 30, 31 (b&l), 33tl, 34, 35, 38, 39, 40, 41, 44, 45, 50, 51, 52, 53, 55t, 57, 58, 65b, 66t, 74, 75, 96 (t&b), 98 (t&b), 100, 101, 104 (t&b), 105, 111, 112, 130, 132, 135br, 137tl, 139, 140, 141, 142, 143 (t), 144, 145b, 147t, 151, 154 (t&b), 156, 161, 162, 164, 166, 167 (t&b), 170, 174 (tr&cl), 176, 177, 180, 181 (t&b), 184, 185, 186, 187 (t&b)
Image Select 60b, 66cl, 108 (t), 110, 116 (l&r), 118, 119, 123r, 128, 133, 139
Israel Government Tourist Organisation 85tr
Japan National Tourist Office 171, 173 (t&b)
Jason Laure 107
Lauros-Giraudon 113
A. Muzzolini 48b
  from *Images rupestres du Sahara* by A. Muzzolini, 1995
Janet Ossebaard 46
Ann Ronan/Image Select 48t, 70, 72, 124t
Paul Sevingy 49
Elena Tchernychko at Kirlian Reseach Ltd.114t, 131
Gerry Thompson 23b
The Travel Library 44, 47, 83tl
Trip 13, 32tr, 33br, 37, 75, 79b, 80, 84bl, 92, 94b, 119, 123cl, 124b, 172b
Courtesy American Heritage, University of Wyoming 16, 17, 24, 25
Anna Watson 168, 169
Nicholas Wood at Sacred Hoop Magazine 78

All other photographs are the copyright of Quarto Publishing plc.

Quarto would also like to thank the AcuMedic Centre, London, for supplying the herbs photographed on page 161.